KU-533-018

Exploring the
LUSITANIA

PEACE·HAS·HER·CONQUESTS·GREATER·FAR·THAN·WAR·

R.M.S.LUSITANIA
QUEEN OF THE SEAS.

Exploring the
LUSITANIA

Probing the Mysteries of the Sinking That Changed History

by Robert D. Ballard *with* Spencer Dunmore

Paintings *by* Ken Marschall ❦ Historical consultation *by* Eric Sauder

A WEIDENFELD AND NICOLSON / MADISON PRESS BOOK

Design and compilation ©1995 Madison Publishing Inc. Text ©1995 Odyssey Corporation and Lonfield Creative Arts Inc.

First published in Great Britain in 1995 by Weidenfeld and Nicolson
The Orion Publishing Group
5 Upper Saint Martin's Lane
London WC2 9EA

All rights reserved. No part of this publication may be reproduced, stored in a retrieval system, or transmitted in any form or by any means, electronic, mechanical, photocopying, recording or otherwise, without the prior permission of the copyright holder.

Dr Robert D. Ballard and Spencer Dunmore have asserted their moral right to be identified as the authors of this work in accordance with the Copyright, Designs and Patents Act 1988.

A catalogue reference is available from the British Library

ISBN 0-297-81314-5

Produced by
Madison Press Books
40 Madison Avenue
Toronto, Ontario
Canada
M5R 2S1

Printed in Italy

Chapter One

The Old Head *of* Kinsale, 1993

THE ROCKY FINGER OF LAND CALLED THE OLD HEAD of Kinsale juts out three miles from the southern coast of Ireland, its lighthouse standing like a sentry at its farthest point. Flanked by the restless sea and swept by its winds, the Old Head is a breathtakingly beautiful spot. My wife, Barbara, and I first saw it the year before, in the summer of 1992, and loved it from the start. I remember strolling along the edge of the steep cliffs toward the lighthouse, gazing out over the sun-dappled sea, savoring the fresh, salty air and reveling in the magnificent scenery. It was hard to believe that one of the great marine tragedies of the century took place only a few miles from where we stood. We could pick out the spot: precisely 11.2 miles south and two degrees west of the lighthouse. I found myself studying the water as if expecting to see something marking the site. There, in 49 fathoms, or 295 feet, a ship called the *Lusitania* died. So did 1,195 passengers and crew.

It happened one May afternoon in 1915. It was an uncommonly lovely day in early spring and warm enough for a family from nearby Bandon to journey to

Today the Old Head of Kinsale on Ireland's southern coast looks much as it did eighty years ago, when the Lusitania *was sunk within sight of its lighthouse.*

T*he* Lusitania's *sinking shocked the world and magazine illustrators competed to convey the horror of it.*

the Old Head for a picnic. Munching on their sandwiches, the picnickers spotted the luxurious four-stacker steaming into view from the southwest. Among the biggest and fastest liners on the Atlantic run, she had sailed nonstop from New York. Her destination was Liverpool. She never arrived. At a few minutes past 2 P.M., while the horrified spectators watched from shore, a torpedo slammed into the liner's starboard side. Seconds later, another, larger explosion staggered the great ship and a huge column of water and debris suddenly erupted out of the sea. A thunderous crack echoed across the sparkling water. Within moments the ship took on a frightening list to starboard. And eighteen minutes later the *Lusitania*, the pride of the Cunard line, had vanished. Hundreds of passengers and crew were left struggling in the frigid water amid a chaotic scum of deck chairs, hatch covers, boxes, bottles, barrels, life jackets and the wreckage of dozens of lifeboats destroyed during frantic but hopeless attempts to launch them from the crazily tilted liner. Of the 1,959 passengers and crew, only 764 survived.

Few events of the Great War shocked the world as profoundly as the sinking of the *Lusitania*. In May 1915 no one believed that sailors of any civilized nation would ever attack an unarmed passenger liner by slinking beneath the surface and torpedoing it without warning. Of the 1,195 who died, 123 of them were Americans, victims of a war in which their country was not involved.

Standing in the sunshine, gazing at that innocent strip of water, I kept wondering about the sinking. The *Lusitania* was a strongly built ship. Although designed primarily as a passenger liner, she could, with minor modifications, be adopted for service as a so-called auxiliary cruiser. At the time of her launching, the press made much of her double bottom and her watertight compartments, describing her as "as unsinkable as a ship can be." Yet the magnificent *Lusitania* went down a mere eighteen minutes after the torpedo struck her. Why didn't she stay afloat at least as long as the *Titanic*, a far less robust vessel? The ill-fated White Star liner remained on the surface for more than two hours after having 250 feet of her hull torn by an iceberg. And why did so many *Lusitania* survivors recall two explosions, when all the records indicate that the German U-boat *U-20* fired only one torpedo?

For years there was speculation that the great Cunarder's mission might not have been as innocent as the British wanted everyone to believe. In defiance of maritime law, some claimed, the luxury liner was being employed to carry high explosives purchased in America for use by the Allies at the front. Not only that, it was rumored that a monstrously cynical conspiracy had precipitated the disaster. The British *wanted* the ship sunk — reasoning that the violent and unprovoked deaths of prominent Americans would bring the United States into the war on the Allied side — and Winston Churchill, the wily First Lord of the Admiralty, was behind it.

Our mission in Ireland was to uncover the truth about the loss of the famous liner, to separate fact from fiction once and for all. Before we set off for Ireland, I was inclined to believe that illegal high explosives in the ship's magazine had probably caused the tragedy. It made perfect sense: the torpedo hits the starboard side of the liner; the explosion ignites the arms and explosives stacked in the ship's magazine and sets off the huge secondary explosion.

But not everything added up. According to survivors' reports, the torpedo hit the ship below or just in front of the bridge. This was well back from the magazine, and a long way for flames or sparks to travel, particularly with sturdy steel bulkheads in the way.

The first dives on the Lusitania *wreck were made in the 1930s. Despite the impression this illustration gives, those early visits took place in almost total darkness.*

Could the ship's huge boilers have been the cause of the catastrophe? The horrific effects of cold seawater coming in contact with red-hot boilers are known to any student of maritime history — an immediate, tremendous explosion. But none of the *Lusitania*'s surviving boiler-room crewmen reported such an explosion. So what really happened?

In the eighty years since the *Lusitania* went down, there have been a number of attempts to solve the mystery. In the mid 1930s, an Englishman, Jim Jarrat, became the first person to stand on the famous ship since May 7, 1915. Trussed up in the heavy, clumsy diving gear of the period, he could see very little due to his equipment and the lack of effective lighting. Hardly surprisingly, he became confused and thought the ship was lying on her port side, not on her starboard side as future divers found. A quarter of a century later, an American diver, John Light, used scuba gear to make a number of dives on the ship. Aided by better lighting than Jim Jarrat had, he confirmed that the *Lusitania* lay on her starboard side. Light reported a gigantic hole in the ship's prow on the port side. He said that the fractured steel plate was bent outward — sure proof, he claimed, that the damage resulted from an internal explosion of tremendous force. Light had no doubt that the U-boat's torpedo set off illegal explosives stacked in the *Lusitania*'s magazine. The result: a catastrophic explosion that blew an immense hole in the hull, causing the rapid plunge of the great liner.

In the early 1980s Oceaneering International set

out to explore the wreck. The firm had been hired by a consortium consisting of press and television interests in the United States and Britain as well as two British engineers who wanted to test their ideas for raising great weights from the depths of the sea. The focus was more on the recovery of the gold bullion and other valuables reportedly entombed in the wreck than in unraveling the mystery of the sinking.

Interestingly, the British government chose to comment on this expedition. The Ministry of Defence in London warned the Oceaneering team that "it would be imprudent not to point out the obvious but real danger inherent if explosives did happen to be present..." Eager readers might have thought they were about to get an admission from an official British source that explosives had indeed been carried on the liner. They were to be disappointed: "The Ministry does not know of any evidence whatsoever that might substantiate rumours of other explosives." In short, look out for explosives, but if you find any, we didn't put them there.

I had long wanted to explore the wreck of the *Lusitania* and find out the truth behind the sinking that shook the world of our great-grandfathers to its complacent foundations. Millions have long regarded it as the event that brought the United States into World War I. It wasn't. Although 123 Americans died in the sinking and uncounted numbers of their compatriots called for an immediate declaration of war, the sinking was little more than one step. Two years would elapse and dozens of angry notes would pass between Washington and Berlin before the United States joined the Allies and went "Over There."

It had always seemed to me that this was much more than the loss of a great ship and many hundreds of lives. The tragedy can be seen as a kind of turning point in our century, marking the abrupt termination of one era and the beginning of another. The sinking itself, tragic though it was, didn't cause any major shift in attitudes, but perhaps it was the last straw, the final shove that sent our world into a moral abyss from which it has still not extricated itself. Back in those innocent

days the foundation of civilized society was a code of conduct that seemed immutable. But one by one the rules began to be bent. Soon conduct mattered less than material gain; more and more, principle yielded to profit. Many would say that the fabric of our society has been steadily unraveling ever since that May day off the Irish coast.

✺

OUR APPROACH TO THE PROBLEM MIGHT BE COMPARED to that of a team of detectives at the scene of a crime. We had the victim, we had evidence, we had testimony from the leading participants. Now it was time to sort it all out and find answers to questions that had been evading historians for eight decades. The big advantage we had over all those who had gone before was advanced technology. Not only did we bring to the job a unique assembly of vehicles, both remotely controlled and manned, but we had also developed a highly efficient method of tracking them. While this may not sound as exciting as some aspects of exploring under the sea, it is actually the key to a successful mission of this type. Visibility is bad in these waters. Powerful lighting is a big help, of course, but only relatively small areas can be seen. For earlier expeditions to the *Lusitania* the overwhelming difficulty had always been to get the big picture. It was like trying to explore the Kennedy Space Center in total darkness with only a flashlight for illumination. No wonder Jim Jarrat got confused; all he could see was a few square feet of steel plate. Other explorers weren't much better equipped to uncover the *Lusitania*'s secrets. Our tracking system would enable us to determine exactly where any of our vehicles were at any time and, equally important, their precise positions on the wreck. All this information would be fed to us in the control room on the command ship and displayed on video screens. With three robot vehicles (*Jason*, *Homer* and *Medea*) plus one manned submersible (*Delta*) in action at any time, the control room would be much like an air traffic center with controllers in charge of the movements — and safety — of several vehicles simultaneously.

We had reassembled the same team that explored

the *Titanic* and the great German battleship *Bismarck*. I'm always fascinated by the chemistry of fine teamwork. Each individual injects his or her personality and point of view, subtly influencing the entire group. Thus the whole becomes far more than the sum of its parts. In our case a melding of talents and expertise had produced a unique team, including Barbara, who handled most of the advance planning for this expedition; salty-tongued Andy Bowen, whose knowledge of *Jason* is equaled only by his experience of the sea (and who possesses an inexhaustible supply of off-color stories); Dana Yoerger, who is as much a master of the computer keyboard as Mozart was of the piano, and who contributed so much to the development of *Jason*; Martin Bowen, ROV (remotely operated vehicle) pilot, whose uncanny ability to find his way about the chaos of the wreck was vital to the success of the expedition; Ken Marschall, the brilliant maritime artist, and historians Eric and Bill Sauder, two of the world's leading *Lusitania* experts. I think all of us felt the same amalgam of emotions: anticipation mingled with apprehension in equal proportions. It is the usual mental state of explorers when the moment of truth approaches. Thrilling discoveries are so often accompanied by crushing disappointments.

While the combined knowledge, skill and experience of our teammates would enable us to reach and explore the wreck in the physical sense, there was another dimension to our mission. I hoped we would all come to understand much more about the age in which the *Lusitania* lived. And that's just what happened. We all began to feel a real kinship with the people involved — the passengers and crew who sailed so blithely into disaster, the writers and politicians in the Allied camp who could barely find words to express their outrage and, yes, the U-boat men who were fighting to break a blockade that threatened to starve their country into submission. The more we explored, the more we were able to see what had happened through their eyes, to share their fears, their anger, their hopes.

(Top) Members of our team confer. (Above) Bill Sauder, Ken Marschall, Eric Sauder and I examine a Lusitania *model.*

(Above left) Our command vessel, Northern Horizon, *riding at anchor off the Irish coast. (Above right) On her after deck,* Delta *and our ROV* Jason *are tethered to the cranes used to raise and lower them during our explorations.*

PRIDE *of the* CUNARD LINE

COMPETITION brought her into being. As the nineteenth century gave way to the twentieth, two developments dominated the lucrative and prestigious transatlantic passenger trade. First, to the dismay of the British, who had enjoyed the lion's share of the business for years, the German lines introduced several excellent and technically advanced liners, including *Kaiser Wilhelm der Grosse* and *Deutschland.* Designed for high-speed crossings, the Germans soon took the Blue Riband, that purely symbolic but highly prized award for the fastest ship on the Atlantic run. Second, and actually more disturbing to the British, the American financier J. Pierpont Morgan acquired control of the White Star Line, Cunard's chief rival. The takeover had troubling implications. For centuries, Britain's merchant marine had been regarded as an auxiliary of the Royal Navy, its ships and seamen readily available in time of war. Could Britain depend on a foreign-owned line to do its duty in

any future national hour of need?

For Cunard, these two facts posed both problems and opportunities. Cunard's chairman, the energetic Lord Inverclyde, approached the government of Arthur Balfour with an idea. He proposed building two technologically advanced superliners, faster, vaster and infinitely more luxurious than anything

else then afloat; what's more, they would be readily adaptable for service as auxiliary cruisers when needed. Inverclyde's proposal was appealing, but it carried a hefty price tag. In order to finance the new ships, Cunard wanted a twenty-year loan of £2,600,000 at a mere 2.75 percent per annum, barely half

(Above) A period postcard showing the Lusitania *under full steam. Such postcards were commonly sold aboard ship as souvenirs. (Right) The* Lusitania *tying up in New York. Her narrow beam, intended for high-speed running, owed more to contemporary warship design than to the style of other liners.*

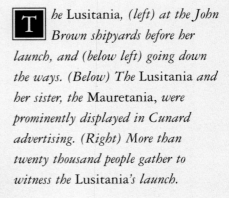

The Lusitania, (left) at the John Brown shipyards before her launch, and (below left) going down the ways. (Below) The Lusitania and her sister, the Mauretania, were prominently displayed in Cunard advertising. (Right) More than twenty thousand people gather to witness the Lusitania's launch.

the going rate. The cost shocked the government, but the idea was too good to turn down. Parliament voted yes.

For naval architect Leonard Peskett, the two new ships represented the biggest challenge of his career. It wasn't enough that they had to be the ultimate ships, they also had to be instantly convertible into warships. But although mountings were provided so that a dozen six-inch quick-firing guns could be added to the liners without difficulty, what use the ships would ever be in battle was questionable. Without armor plate and with prodigious appetites for coal, they would be about as useful in a modern-day sea battle as thoroughbreds at a plowing match.

Soon, amid the acrid stink and the mind-numbing din of the shipyards, two stupendous vessels began to take shape: the 785-foot-long *Lusitania* at the John Brown yards at Clydebank in Scotland, and her 790-foot-long sister ship, *Mauretania*, at the Swan Hunter and Wigham Richardson yards, at Newcastle-upon-Tyne in northern England. Both liners had a displacement of about forty-thousand tons. Powered by the biggest, most powerful marine steam turbines ever, they combined lithe good looks with performance, promising a top speed of over twenty-five knots with capacity for more

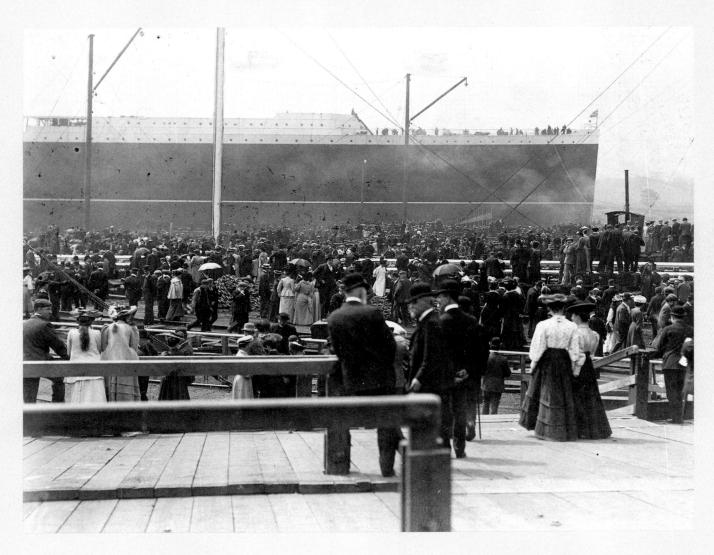

than two thousand passengers and a crew of some 850. There could be no doubt that the two glamorous sisters would recapture the Blue Riband for Britain.

The *Lusitania* was the first to be launched, on June 6, 1906. Sadly, Lord Inverclyde didn't live to see the great ship become a reality. He had died suddenly the year before at the age of forty-four. His widow, Mary, christened the *Lusitania,* watched by a throng of some

twenty thousand, including invited guests and much of the population of Clydebank. Sir Charles MacLaren, John Brown's deputy chairman, put the whole project on a patriotic, if not chauvinistic plane by declaring that "Great Britain, as mistress of the sea and leader in marine construction" could never have rested until Germany's hold on the Blue Riband was broken. Further, he noted, with "slight" alterations, the ship could

become "the fastest and most powerful cruiser in the world."

&

It took a year to fit *Lusitania* out, to install the huge turbines, the boilers, the refrigerating equipment, the dish-washing machinery, the thousands of items of furniture, the countless boxes and bales, crates and cartons of everything from lubricating oil to toilet rolls. Eventually, she had only to undergo her final sea trials before being handed over to Cunard. No one doubted that she would pass with flying colors.

She didn't.

To their horror, the engineers discovered that the splendid ship, the nation's darling, had a vice: her stern vibrated at high speed. And in keeping with the epic character of the ship, the *Lusitania*'s was no delicate trembling but a violent shuddering, a convulsion that rattled through her steel plates and girders, her strakes and stanchions, rendering much of the stern of the ship unusable. The builders had no choice: they gutted the entire section, home of 142 second-class cabins, and added an assortment of arches, brackets, gussets, pillars, items of built-in furniture, and any other handy form of bracing. The work took a month and was horrendously costly, but it had to be done.

At last, newly trussed, the *Lusitania* set off on her maiden voyage to New York in September 1907. The occasion generated an orgy of hyberbole by the press. Her size and splendid proportions dazzled reporters. She was, as just about every journalist dutifully reported, the largest

movable object ever built by Man. It took more than twenty trains to carry the five thousand tons of coal she needed to take her across the Atlantic, powered by her huge turbines with their three million meticulously machined blades. Some 65,000 gallons of water *per minute* were needed to keep the engines cool. Four million rivets were used during construction; in all, they weighed five hundred tons. No less than 250 miles of cable snaked through her innards, supplying electrical power for everything from dozens of clocks and lamps to motors for cooking, dough-mixing, ice-cream freezing, and boot-cleaning. Electrical power opened and closed her thirty-four major watertight compartments, the "steel honeycomb" that would have saved her had she been involved in a collision of the sort that later sank *Titanic*. She was, declared the *New York Times* confidently, "as unsinkable as a ship can be..."

Surrounded by smaller vessels, the Lusitania *steams into New York in September 1907 at the completion of her maiden voyage from Liverpool.*

Chapter Two

The 202*nd* Crossing

May 1, 1915, Pier 54, New York

I T WOULD BE A BUSY DAY. SAILING DAYS ALWAYS were, with hundreds of passengers to be processed and boarded, thousands of pieces of luggage to be sorted into what was needed on the voyage and what wasn't. There would be a huge crowd to see the great ship off. New Yorkers had taken her to their hearts from the day she first arrived on her maiden voyage eight years before. Since then she had tied up in New York more than a hundred times. She was a familiar sight at the foot of Fourteenth Street in the malodorous heart of the meat-packing district, looming over the other liners, making them look insignificant and unimportant.

But there was another reason for a big turnout of New Yorkers on this day. The ship would be carrying an unusually large number of American citizens on this voyage, the largest number since the war in Europe had flared up a few months before.

To fuel the Lusitania, or (left and below) her sister, the Mauretania, barges were brought alongside and coal was dumped through doors in her side, into the bunkers. (Bottom left and right) Before sailing, the ship's stokers busily fed the ship's dozens of giant boilers.

She was the RMS *Lusitania*.

Preparations for departure had begun long before the first passengers set foot on a gangway. Coal, more than five thousand tons of it, had slithered and slammed down chutes into the bunkers. Coaling was a dirty business; after it was completed, the decks had to be thoroughly hosed down and the brasses polished until they glittered like mirrors. The smell of coal dust and lubricating oil added their distinctive piquance to the fishy breezes as the loading of cargo began. Although designed principally to carry passengers and their baggage, the ship had room for some freight. On this trip, the hold would accommodate loads of copper and brass; packing cases filled with machine tools and dental equipment; 350,000 pounds of beef, lard and bacon; 205 barrels of Connecticut oysters; 25 cases of oil, and dozens of boxes of this and that. The cargo was valued at $750,000, according to the manifest approved by U.S. Customs.

For weeks German agents had been circulating rumors that the passengers aboard the *Lusitania* would be accompanied by contraband: tons of high explosive destined for the war fronts. The rumormongers had it all wrong. Although the cargo included 4,200 cases of .303-caliber rifle ammunition purchased from the Remington Company, the bullets were perfectly legal cargo. Officials had conducted a series of tests some years before the war, subjecting boxes of cartridges to rough treatment and to open fires without dangerous consequences. Thereafter the Department of Commerce and Labor in Washington had declared that small-arms ammunition might be legally transported on passenger liners. And the fact of the matter was, the ship didn't have room for massive supplies of explosives. Although she was among the biggest liners on the Atlantic run, her prime role was to carry passengers and their luggage, not cargo.

Far below the waterline, the black gang labored, thrusting shovelfuls of coal into furnaces, building up the pressure in the boilers. They were a rough bunch, those grimy denizens of the ship's bowels, and most of

A luggage wagon, with the Lusitania's *name clearly marked on the front, pulls up in front of the Cunard pier in New York City.*

them felt out of sorts after spending their shore leave washing away the dust and the dirt of the westward trip with copious quantities of anything alcoholic. Soon the heat in the boiler rooms would become searing; hands would be blistered and blackened. The noise was already enough to make sore heads spin.

Something else contributed to the unease in the boiler rooms. Dowie, the four-year-old black cat, the stokers' mascot, had deserted during the night.

A bad omen, the men claimed.

SIXTEEN-YEAR-OLD CHRISSIE AITKEN WOKE ABRUPTLY, wondering for a moment where she was and what day it was. She had dozed, although it couldn't have been for more than a few minutes. Nevertheless the dream felt as if it taken hours to unfold. She could still feel the shock of it: the train wheezing and whistling to a stop and the man in the peaked cap saying they were too late. The ship had gone, he announced with a shrug.

Vamoosed. The next moment she and her family were standing on the dock clutching suitcases and bags of everything from chocolate bars to tins of baby powder, watching the ship puff away, siren shrieking.

Chrissie opened her eyes. No ship. No dock. The train still rumbled along. Her father, her brother Jarvie, and her brother's young son still sat in the same seats, their heads nodding in time with the train's swaying. The scenery had changed, though. Forest and scrub had at last given way to grubby, untidy city streets, with washing fluttering like flags in the breeze and hordes of people swarming about.

"Are we here?"

"Aye." Her father smiled. He looked tired. Was it any wonder? Four days on a train was enough to wear out any man, even one with a healthy heart. Chrissie prayed that this endless journey hadn't made him sicker than he already was. Why couldn't her father trust a heart specialist on the North American continent? In Vancouver, perhaps, or Seattle. In both cities, there were experts just as competent as the man in Edinburgh. Perhaps even more so. She had said as much to her father, but she might have saved her breath. He clicked his tongue and gave her that familiar you're-too-young-to-understand glance. And that was the end of it. If the ticker needed adjusting, he wanted it adjusted in Scotland. Privately Chrissie believed that her father's heart problem was an excuse. He simply wanted to go to Scotland. Although he had lived in Canada for years, he still yearned for the heather. And so they had set off on this odyssey, all the way from British Columbia right across the continent, through thousands of miles of mountains and featureless prairie. But when they arrived in New York, they found that the Admiralty had commandeered their

After two weeks in the United States, Margaret Mackworth (top) was returning to England with her father (above), the British businessman D.A. Thomas.

ship, the *Cameronia*, to carry troops. With barely an apology — "It's the war, y'know" — the family was assured that space had been reserved for them on another liner.

Chrissie sometimes felt as if all the responsibilities that had been her late mother's had now become hers. These unthinking, impatient males were now her charges, from her father to her infant nephew. She had to look out for them. Why, she wondered, did the daughter of the house always seem to be saddled with more responsibility than the males? It was unfair. Just like a lot of other things in life, she was beginning to discover.

Her thoughts were interrupted by her brother. It didn't trouble Jarvie that they had been bumped from the *Cameronia*. All he could talk about was that fate had snatched them from an ordinary ship and had put them on the world's greatest liner, the *Lusitania*.

❧

MARGARET MACKWORTH TRIED NOT TO gape. But she had an uneasy feeling that her mouth had actually dropped open as she looked up for the first time at the vastness of the hull and the four funnels that seemed to reach up into the very sky. None of the pictures she had seen did the ship justice. Her dimensions were mere numbers on the page; you had to be in the presence of the vessel to appreciate such size. Looming over Margaret was a black field of steel with a bumper crop of rivet heads lined up in meticulous ranks. No wonder the *Lusitania*'s launching nine years before had inspired such enthusiasm in the press. The world's biggest, fastest, most luxurious vessel the papers called her, the incredible floating palace embodying every technological wonder known to man. To dramatize her size, the British magazine *The Sphere* had set the vast liner

(Above) The Lusitania's *enclosed bridge was the preserve of* the ship's captain, William Turner.

upright on her shapely stern beside London's St. Paul's Cathedral. The tip of the cross on the famous dome reached only about halfway up the liner's huge hull.

"I'm afraid there's a bit of a delay," Margaret's father announced, emerging from the dockside office. "Not long. Two or three hours, they say. Extra passengers from the *Cameronia*."

The scene on the Cunard dock reminded Margaret of a Broadway opening night she had witnessed the week before: the same forest of faces, the excited burble of voices, plus the smells of sea and oil and the evocative sounds of the immense ship coming to life.

Margaret had been in America for two weeks. An attractive woman in her early thirties, she was the daughter of the internationally renowned mine owner and entrepreneur David Thomas. Her father had preceded her to America by ten days, his briefcase bulging with documents about Pennsylvania coal mines, barge services on the Mississippi, railways in northern Canada, mining properties and oil fields. He had extensive business interests in North America and for years had traveled across the Atlantic as regularly as some New Yorkers took the Staten Island ferry. It had been fun visiting New York with him, and Margaret was grateful that he had asked her along. Despite early doubts, Margaret had found New York to be a glittering haven of excitement and laughter, a warm and wonderful place after a winter in wartime England. Perhaps she should consider staying longer. Her marriage to Sir Humphrey Mackworth had lasted seven years. She doubted it would last seven more. What then? In her stratum of society divorce was still fairly uncommon.

⁓

FROM HIS VANTAGE POINT ON THE BRIDGE, THE *Lusitania*'s skipper watched the hectic activity on the foredeck below. Captain William Turner had seen the same scene a thousand times. It was always the same just before sailing: too much to do and not enough time to do it. Passengers were already streaming up the gangways. There were a lot of big names among them, according to the Cunard office. Turner shrugged. He wasn't much interested in so-called celebrities — the actors and politicians, the tycoons and the titled. He had never heard of most of them, and he didn't particularly care to know who mattered and who didn't. If the truth were told, he would probably have preferred to carry shiploads of iron castings. Iron castings didn't expect to be entertained. They didn't keep asking half-witted questions about weather or the ship, neither did they complain about the temperature of the morning tea. In many ways bad weather was a blessing; it provided the perfect excuse to stay on the bridge and leave the entertaining and the flattering to those officers with a talent for it.

The fifty-nine-year-old Turner had reached the pinnacle of his profession. He had left home and gone to sea at thirteen, a skinny lad with nothing to offer but a willingness to learn. He was bright enough, but no one could have predicted that he would ever rise to command the finest liner in the world. How had he done it? Luck, partly; he would be the last one to deny it. You had to be at the right place at the right time if you were to get anywhere. Nevertheless, nose-to-the-grindstone hard work had been largely responsible. Turner loved and feared the sea. He knew its moods and its caprices. He knew when it had to be obeyed without question and when it would forgive a few liberties. His was the knowledge of experience, of near-fatal errors, of blind, stupid luck, the sort that stuck with you forever, far better than the stuff that came out of books, in his opinion.

Business seemed to be brisk, Turner noted

approvingly. The outbreak of war the previous August had slashed bookings, and all through the winter traffic had been dismal. But now that spring had arrived, the travelers seemed to be on the move again. Today, May Day, was the busiest in months. No fewer than four major liners would be sailing out of New York. Of these, the biggest and proudest was the *Lusitania*. Then there was the *New York* of the American Line, the *Rotterdam* of the Holland-America Line and Norwegian-America's *Bergensfjord*. Few of the hundreds of passengers strolling up the gangways seemed to see any reason why the war should interfere with their travel plans. Wars were the business of armies and governments. Civilians stood on the sidelines, so to speak, while their soldiers took to the field and their politicians negotiated. The conflict between Britain and her allies and the Central Powers had been raging for nearly ten months. Although there had been reports of the sinking of cargo ships, it was unthinkable that a passenger liner might suffer a similar fate, particularly one with scores of Americans on board. War zones and blockades involved cargo ships and contraband, not passenger liners. Submarines? Like most merchant skippers of his generation, Turner was of the opinion that the Admiralty made far too much of the danger they posed, forever sending reams of directives on how to deal with them. Turner already knew. Outrun the nasty, sneaky things. Or turn and ram them. Slice them open. In Turner's opinion, no skipper commanding a vessel with a strong bow and a good turn of speed need lose any sleep over submarines.

If any passengers expressed concern about the danger from submarines, Turner always told them about the *Lusitania*'s phenomenal speed and how it was the best possible insurance against the wretched contraptions. He kept to himself the fact that Cunard had ordered him to close down six of the ship's boilers, representing some 25 percent of her capacity. It was an economy move. Coal was expensive, and with the war Cunard was barely breaking even with the *Lusitania*. Reducing the number of boilers in use shaved several knots off the liner's top speed, but she was still fast enough to outpace any submarine, or so Cunard's board of directors had assured each other.

Earlier that morning Turner had been told about a message the Germans had put in the newspapers, warning passengers of the dangers of traveling across the ocean in wartime. He had searched his copy of the *New York Times*, wading through page after page of advertisements — for Lord and Taylor (men's spring suits for $17.50), Gimbel Brothers (a Victrola for a mere $7 down and $6 a month), for Hardman and Peck (grand pianos for $650, endorsed by Caruso, no less). Straw hats, false teeth, cures for pimples and piles, falling hair and fallen arches... everybody in New York had something to sell you. At last Turner had found it: a small notice, black-bordered like a death announcement. Prospective travelers "intending to embark on the Atlantic voyage" were reminded that a state of war existed between Germany and her allies and Great Britain and her allies. Journeys were undertaken at passengers' own risk.

Notice or no notice, the Cunard office reported no more than the usual number of last-minute cancellations. According to the paper, the Cunard agent dismissed the warning as just another attempt "to annoy the line and make its passengers uncomfortable."

Turner was impatient to get away. Since the outbreak of war, New York had acquired an odd aura of unreality for him. While untold thousands of brave young men (including his own two sons, Norman and Percy) were fighting to the death in stinking trenches, New Yorkers reckoned the most important event on the planet was the Yankees leading the American League.

ADVERTISEMENT.

NOTICE!

TRAVELLERS intending to embark on the Atlantic voyage are reminded that a state of war exists between Germany and her allies and Great Britain and her allies; that the zone of war includes the waters adjacent to the British Isles; that, in accordance with formal notice given by the Imperial German Government, vessels flying the flag of Great Britain, or of any of her allies, are liable to destruction in those waters and that travellers sailing in the war zone on ships of Great Britain or her allies do so at their own risk.

IMPERIAL GERMAN EMBASSY
WASHINGTON, D. C., APRIL 22, 1915.

This announcement appeared on the same page of the New York newspapers as the Cunard advertisement announcing the Lusitania's scheduled departure.

PASSENGERS CONTINUED TO STREAM ABOARD THE GREAT ship, segregated by class before they even stepped off the dock. Those holding first-class tickets (called "saloon" by Cunard) made their way aboard the ship by one gangway, those heading for second class (Cunard preferred "second cabin") by another and those bound for third class (once known as steerage because on many ships the passengers traveling on the cheapest tickets found themselves in the stern, close to the ship's steering mechanism) by yet another. But even if for some reason you didn't know what class you were traveling in, your treatment by Cunard's cabin staff would soon tell you. First-class passengers were the aristocracy. They had paid for service and they got it. Wallets were quietly opened at the beginning of a voyage and the first installment of the mandatory tips changed hands. Five- and ten-pound notes, ten- and twenty-dollar bills, francs, pesetas, rupees, drachmas: the staff had no trouble converting any currency or instantly classifying any passenger as to social worth.

In second cabin relations between passengers and staff suggested a quietly satisfactory business arrangement between equals. Second-cabin travelers were regarded by the staff as eminently solid citizens who could afford good service; in fact, many of them could afford to travel first class. But the considerably less formal atmosphere in second had its appeal for some. Besides, the wrong accent or questionable family origins could be embarrassing encumbrances in the rarefied atmosphere of first class. In 1915 it was important to know your place. Second-class passengers received every courtesy (provided they tipped well) and, on a ship of *Lusitania's* caliber, could have as comfortable and enjoyable a trip as first-class passengers on any other line.

Third-class passengers were several notches down the social scale as far as the staff was concerned. They were the ship's peasants, largely drawn from the poor of every land in Europe. Seeking a better life in the United States, they filled the ship's third class on the westbound run; returning to the Old World, either to visit or resettle, they filled the same spaces when the ship headed east. In a world that worshipped wealth, they were poor, but their numbers made them the line's bread and butter. Cunard stuffed them in, but treated them well by the standards of the time — although some complained that the cabin staff were worse snobs than the passengers traveling in first class.

❧

THE *LUSITANIA*'S PASSENGER LISTS had featured the names of international celebrities over the years, and this voyage was no exception. Alfred Gwynne Vanderbilt, the thirty-seven year-old multimillionaire sportsman, had booked passage in order to attend a meeting of the International Horse Breeders' Association. The 1914 meeting had been peremptorily canceled because of the outbreak of war. All members had agreed that nothing should prevent this year's meeting from taking place; important matters had to be discussed.

Alfred Vanderbilt had received a mysterious unsigned message at his hotel the previous evening. The *Lusitania* was earmarked for destruction. He ignored the anonymous message, regarding it as a joke in poor taste. The great-grandson of Commodore Vanderbilt, the notorious tycoon who had built up a fabulous empire of railroads and shipping interests, Alfred customarily spent almost as much time in Europe as he did in America. He looked forward to an

Theater producer Charles Frohman was headed for London to check out that season's crop of new plays.

agreeable stay in England, a stimulating combination of business and pleasure. A popular figure at the sporting events, spas and resorts patronized by the well-heeled of the world, Alfred loved the fastest horses, the fastest automobiles and, some said, the fastest women, too. There were rumors that although Alfred was unquestionably going to attend the meeting of the breeders' association, he had a number of other discreet appointments planned, out of the range of prying reporters.

Life had been extraordinarily good to Alfred. The refreshing thing about him was that he seemed to know it, if the breezy shots in the rotogravure sections were anything to go by. He had inherited some $50 million on his father's death and had been busy spending it ever since. Everything he did cost the earth. When he divorced his first wife, Elsie, it set him back a cool $10 million. Fortune had been beaming down on him since the day he drew his first breath. She hadn't stopped yet, it seemed. Three years earlier he had booked passage to New York on the *Titanic*'s maiden voyage. Business had forced him to change his plans at the last moment, and the doomed ship had gone on its way without him.

Charles Frohman, the noted theatrical impresario, was on his way to London to see the current crop of West End productions and decide if any had potential for Broadway. He was also said to have been warned not to sail aboard the *Lusitania*, but like Vanderbilt, he scoffed at the warning. The vastly successful Frohman was often referred to as "the Napoleon of the Drama" because of the power he wielded and because, with his short, stocky build and his dark, intense features, he looked a little like the French leader. Frohman visited London at least once a year, although recently the trips

The Lusitania's *finest cabins were the regal suites, which featured large bedrooms (above) and sitting rooms (below).*
The Lusitania's *combination of luxury and speed attracted such passengers as millionaire Alfred Vanderbilt (below right).*

F or a second-class passenger like Avis Dolphin (left), sailing on the Lusitania *meant a comfortable shared cabin (opposite and above) and cozy public rooms (top) where one could pass the waking hours.*

had become increasingly difficult because of the articular rheumatism that had plagued him since a bad fall some years before. Occasionally the sea air seemed to help the condition; often it only made it worse. Frohman had ordered his passage booked on the *Lusitania* because she was the fastest ship on the Atlantic and he wanted the trip over and done with as rapidly as possible. At one point he had briefly considered sending someone else to London to view the productions and make the decisions, but the truth was, he didn't trust anyone else's judgment. His remarkable success on Broadway had been entirely due to his own ideas and intuition.

Many other passengers' reasons for traveling that day reflected the same lack of worry about the war and its dangers. Englishman Stewart Mason had just married Leslie, the daughter of a prominent Boston manufacturer, William Lindsay. The journey to Britain aboard the *Lusitania* was to be their honeymoon. Twelve-year-old Avis Dolphin was going to Britain to attend school. Her mother, the proprietor of a nursing home in St. Thomas, Ontario, was determined that her daughter should have an English education. As it happened, a nurse, one of Mrs. Dolphin's employees, was visiting England, and she had agreed to look after Avis on the trip. Avis looked forward to seeing the homeland she had left at the age of two when her parents emigrated.

Others had sterner purposes for sailing that day. Elbert Hubbard, the famed "Sage of East Aurora," intended to interview Kaiser Wilhelm. Hubbard was the author of the best-selling novel *Message to Garcia* and the publisher of the monthly magazine *The Philistine*, a flamboyant man who wore long hair and floppy bow ties. He had met the German emperor in happier days, and although he had since written some uncomplimentary things about Germany, he was optimistic about his chances of scoring a journalistic coup.

Like many expatriate Britons, Oliver Bernard wanted to enlist in his country's armed forces. A talented theatrical designer, he had been working in

Boston, Massachusetts, when war broke out. He hurried back to England, but the army turned him down; so did the Royal Flying Corps and the Royal Naval Air Service. His hearing was not up to the required standard, the doctors informed him bleakly. Swallowing his disappointment, Bernard returned to his job at the Boston Opera House. It paid well and he liked Boston and Bostonians, but the feeling that he should be doing something for his country in its time of trial still nagged at him. When a friend in London wrote that the forces had become less particular about minor medical shortcomings in recruits, he lost no time in arranging his passage. He wanted to get to England as soon as possible. The *Lusitania* was the obvious choice.

❧

IN THEIR THIRD-CLASS CABIN THE WILLIAMS FAMILY arranged their belongings. It didn't take long. They

had little more than the clothes they stood in. Everything that could be sold had been disposed of to pay for steamship tickets. When that hadn't been enough, good-hearted neighbors in Plainfield, New Jersey, had come up with the rest. The family's immigration to America some years earlier had been a disaster. No sooner had they all arrived in America than the head of the family, John Williams, deserted them. They believed he had gone back to England, but they weren't sure. In any event, Mrs. Williams and her six children had little choice but to go there and hope that somehow things would work themselves out. Accompanying Annie Williams were nine-year-old Edith and the younger children — Edward, George, Florence, Ethel and four-month-old David. It was a tight squeeze in the cabin, but they didn't complain. This journey was going to be the start of better times for the family, they were sure of it.

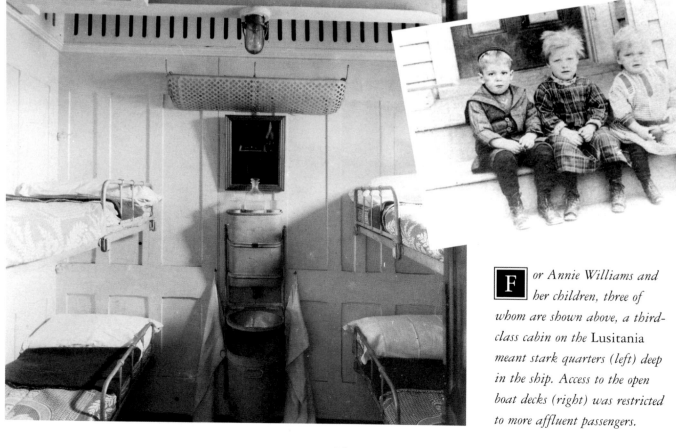

F or Annie Williams and her children, three of whom are shown above, a third-class cabin on the Lusitania meant stark quarters (left) deep in the ship. Access to the open boat decks (right) was restricted to more affluent passengers.

IT WAS NOW NEARLY NOON AND BOARDING HAD almost been completed. Saloon (first-class) passengers totaled 291 — by no means a full complement (the ship could accommodate 552 in saloon) but quite respectable, considering the times. Second cabin was bulging at its metallic seams, with 601 passengers in space originally intended for 460; however, the unusually large number of infants eased the squeeze to a degree, since many were sharing with their parents. Third class was the real surprise: only 373 in a space designed for 1,186.

❧

RUMORS HAD CIRCULATED FOR WEEKS THAT THE Germans were bent on destroying the *Lusitania*, the pride of Britain's mercantile fleet. Some said the attempt would be made while she was in port, probably in New York, because it would be far easier for saboteurs to enter than Liverpool. Cunard tightened security at Pier 54. Guards patrolled the area twenty-four hours a day. No one got on or off the ship without proper authorization. Some said the Germans wouldn't try anything in port but would have a swarm of submarines lying in wait for her somewhere on her transatlantic route. The times and dates of her sailing were no mystery; all the major newspapers carried listings.

As far as most of the *Lusitania*'s passengers were concerned, however, this was just another sailing. Unlike Alfred Vanderbilt and Charles Frohman, they had received no warnings from persons unknown; they knew nothing about German threats to sink the ship. They expected a pleasant spring voyage.

❧

THE DAY BEFORE THE *LUSITANIA* WAS DUE TO SAIL FROM New York, a submarine slipped out of the port of Emden on Germany's north coast and headed northwest. The figure 20 on the vessel's bow identified her

Chapter Three

The Last Departure

B ENEATH HER STERN THE SLUGGISH HUDSON
River frothed as the turbines began to turn
the ship's massive propellers. To witness the
Lusitania moving away from the dock was like seeing a
city block breaking free of its foundations. Hundreds
of passengers lined the rails, waving, taking photographs, some laughing, others weeping.

In midstream three tugs puffed up to the *Lusitania*.

Like playful cubs clustering around their mother, they nudged and coaxed her bow until it was pointing downstream. There she was at last, one of the biggest, fastest liners on the Atlantic run, ready to set sail for Europe, war or no war. She was a proud and beautiful statement of British confidence.

On the dock and on the ship, forests of hands still waved, fluttering handkerchiefs like tiny flags. People strained to keep friends and family in view as long as possible. But gradually faces became little pink blobs, indistinguishable from one another. The handkerchiefs vanished one by one. The stevedores turned away, already dismissing the *Lusitania* from their minds. She had gone; now there were other ships to worry about.

Aboard the great liner, the passengers on deck began to disperse. It had become noticeably cooler since the ship had pulled away from the dock. New York passed before their eyes, the thriving, striving city, brash and crude, yet throbbing with ideas and opportunities. Margaret Mackworth found herself in the classic dilemma of the traveler: she longed to be back in her native Wales, yet she was genuinely sad to be leaving. New York had broadened her horizons just as much as

H arbor tugs push the great liner's bow into proper position, facing downriver (below). To make her harder for German ships to identify, the stacks have been painted black and the brass letters on the bow covered up. (Previous page) The Lusitania sitting at dock in happier, prewar times, with both the ship and the Cunard pier festooned with flags.

Beneath the grand dome, the first-class dining room featured Corinthian columns, potted palms and (left) a menu with a range of satisfying fare.

The Lounge,
s.s. LUSITANIA.

4029

ON BOARD THE
CUNARD
R.M.S "LUSITANIA"

ON BOARD THE
CUNARD
R.M.S "LUSITANIA"

ON BOARD THE
CUNARD
R.M.S "LUSITANIA"

T he sumptuous lounge (above) vied with the first-class dining room for the title of the liner's most elegant showpiece. Its stained-glass ceiling was lit with skylights by day and by electric bulbs at night. Refreshments were served to passengers who played cards or conversed in the cosy groupings of chairs. A mostly female retreat (right), was the reading and writing room, where one could dash off a note on Lusitania stationery (left).

TONNAGE 33,000.   HORSE POWER 70,000.   SPEED 25 KNOTS.

LOUNGE.   (CUNARD LINE.)

R.M.S. "LUSITANIA."   SMOKING ROOM.

The color scheme of the lounge is conveyed by this period postcard (top) while another postcard (above) depicts the first-class smoking room. This was an exclusively male haunt, as was the ship's barbershop (below).

I n warmer weather, first-class passengers could gather in the verandah café (above and below). One side of the restaurant could be opened up on good days to create the seagoing equivalent of a sidewalk café.

VERANDAH CAFE, LUSITANIA AND MAURETANIA.

T he airy feel of the verandah café was carried over into other parts of the ship, such as the grand entrance (left) on the boat deck.

SECOND CLASS

A lthough plainer, the dining room for the Lusitania's second-class passengers (above) echoed that of first class, even featuring an open well over the middle of the room. Thanks to the Lusitania's size, these public rooms were larger and more handsomely appointed than the first-class quarters on many smaller ships. The selection of food available (right) assured that no second-class passenger would go hungry.

CUNARD LINE

SECOND CABIN.

R.M.S. "LUSITANIA."

FRIDAY, SEPTEMBER 19th, 1913.

: : BREAKFAST. : :

Apples   Figs
Oatmeal Porridge and Fresh Milk
Fried Whiting   Smoked Herrings
Fried and Turned Eggs
Savoury Omelettes (to order)
Broiled Wiltshire Bacon   Saute of Liver
Grilled Beef Steak with Tomatoes
Saute Potatoes
Rice Cakes, Golden Syrup
White & Graham Rolls   Scotch Scones
Vienna Bread
Marmalade   Jam
Tea   Coffee   Cocoa

SECOND CABIN

R.M.S. "LUSITANIA."

SUNDAY, OCTOBER 4th. 1908.

MENU.

Bouilli Soup
Boiled Hake, Anchovy Sauce
Spaghetti, Italienne   Curried Mutton with Rice
Roast Beef, Browned Potatoes
Boiled Chicken, Parsley Sauce
Corned Leg of Pork, Vegetables
Boiled Rice
Cabbage   Boiled Potatoes
Wine Jelly   Small Pastry
Apple Tart   Plum Pudding, Sweet Sauce
Ice Cream
Cheese   Dessert
Tea   Coffee

O ther second-class public rooms included the ladies' drawing room (right), which in this picture rather inexplicably features more men than women. (Below) A souvenir paperweight sold in the Lusitania's barber shop.

A ll of the second-class public rooms were located toward the stern of the ship, in a deckhouse that was physically separated from the areas reserved for first-class passengers farther forward. The lounge (right) was located on the top deck of the after deckhouse and gave a view of the sea through its windows. (Below right) Second-class passengers gather on the promenade deck, just outside the lounge.

THIRD CLASS

In third class, there were no
pretensions toward making
the ship look like a hotel or country
house. The highly functional nature
of third class is evident from the

CUNARD LINE

LUSITANIA
MAURETANIA
CAMPANIA

LIVERPOOL
QUEENSTOWN
NEW YORK

THIRD CLASS

SPECIMEN THIRD CLASS BILLS OF FARE

	BREAKFAST.	DINNER.	TEA.
Sunday	Oatmeal Porridge and Milk or Syrup. Tight and Hard Boiled Eggs. Irish Stew. Bread and Butter. Jam or Marmalade. Tea or Coffee.	Soup. Roast Beef. Vegetables and Potatoes. Bread. Plum Pudding. Sweet Sauce. Fresh Fruit.	Tea. Mutton Chops. Bunloaf. Bread & Butter. Jam or Marmalade.
Monday	Oatmeal Porridge and Milk or Syrup. Fried Fresh Fish. Broiled Beef Steak. Bread and Butter. Jam or Marmalade. Tea or Coffee.	Soup. Mutton Hot Pot. Potatoes and Vegetables. Rice Pudding. Bread.	Tea. Boiled Eggs. Stewed Apricots and Rice. Bread and Butter. Jam or Marmalade.
Tuesday	Oatmeal Porridge and Milk or Syrup. Spiced Herrings. Hot Roast Mutton. Potatoes. Bread and Butter. Jam or Marmalade. Tea or Coffee.	Pea Soup. Boiled Beef. Vegetables and Potatoes. Stewed Prunes and Rice. Bread. Fresh Fruit.	Tea. Fried Fresh Fish. Bread and Butter. Jam or Marmalade.
Wednesday	Oatmeal Porridge and Milk or Syrup. Steak and Onions. Corned Beef. Dry Hash. Potatoes. Bread and Butter. Tea or Coffee. Jam or Marmalade.	Roast Pork and Apple Sauce. Potatoes and Green Peas. Suet Pudding. Bread. Pickles.	Tea. Corned Beef. Cheese. Bread & Butter. Jam or Marmalade.
Thursday	Oatmeal Porridge and Milk or Syrup. Irish Stew. Curried Veal and Rice. Bread and Butter. Jam or Marmalade.	Soup. Steak & Kidney Pie. Potatoes. Vegetables. Sago Pudding. Bread. Pickles.	Tea. Broiled Sausages. Stewed Apples and Rice. Bread & Butter. Jam or Marmalade.
Friday	Oatmeal Porridge and Milk or Syrup. Salt Herrings. Liver and Bacon. Potatoes. Bread and Butter. Jam or Marmalade. Tea or Coffee.	Soup. Ling Fish and Egg Sauce. Mutton Stew. Potatoes. Vegetables. Bread and Butter. Plum Pudding. Fresh Fruit	Tea. Fish Cakes. Bread & Butter. Jam or Marmalade.
Saturday	Oatmeal Porridge and Milk or Syrup. Steak and Onions. Potatoes. Savoury Omelette. Bread and Butter. Jam or Marmalade. Tea or Coffee.	Soup. Boiled Mutton. Caper Sauce. Potatoes. Vegetables. Stewed Prunes and Rice. Bread. Pickles	Tea. Corned Beef. Dry Hash. Currant Buns. Bread & Butter. Jam or Marmalade.

Supper Daily. — Gruel at 8 p.m. if required. Chicken Broth, Beef Tea, and Jellies supplied to Invalids when required. Special Milk supplied to Infants and Invalids as required, also Scandinavian Bread, supplied to Third Class Passengers. The best quality of Cabin Bread.

The Bills of Fare are varied daily at the discretion of the Chief Steward.

Special attention is paid to the supplying of extra comforts for Women and Children and those who are sick.

The Provisions supplied are of the very best quality. They are examined when put on board by His Majesty's Medical Emigration Officers.

brochure that Cunard issued (left). Everything from the companionways (top right) to the smoking room (upper right) and the ladies' sitting room (lower right), to the vast dining saloon (above and bottom right, in use) has the same bare bones look, designed for hard use and ease of upkeep.

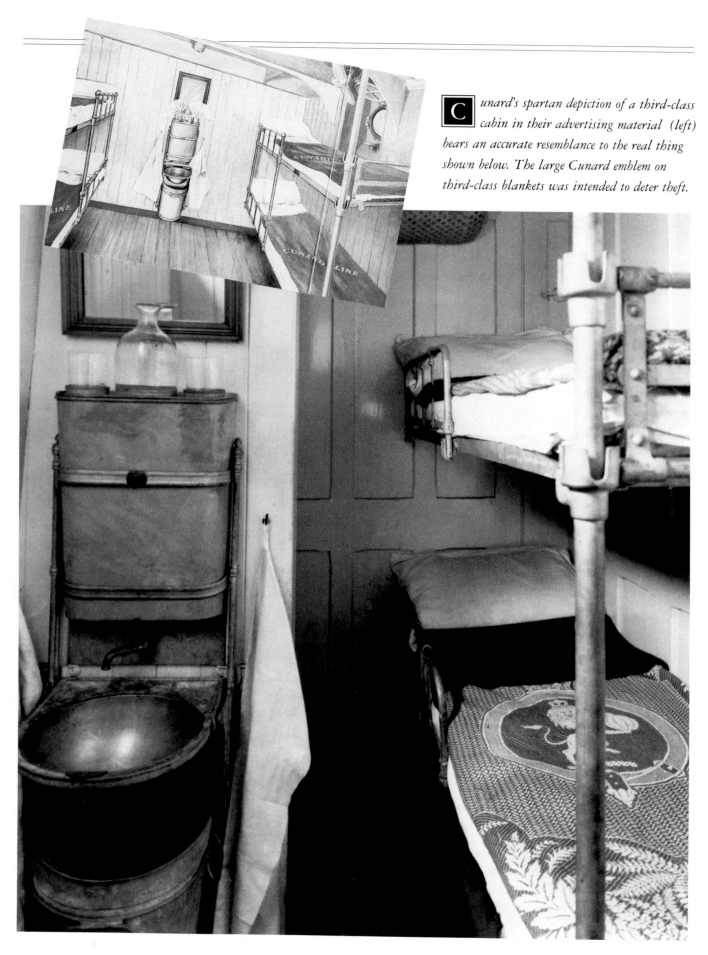

unard's spartan depiction of a third-class cabin in their advertising material (left) bears an accurate resemblance to the real thing shown below. The large Cunard emblem on third-class blankets was intended to deter theft.

CHRISSIE AITKEN WAS OBLIGED TO SHARE HER SECOND-class cabin with a tall, rather forbidding-looking woman of about thirty. She seemed preoccupied and little interested in small talk, so Chrissie said nothing as she unpacked her suitcase amid the rumbling of the ship's engines and the chatter and clatter of people in the corridor. The cabin was as beautiful as everything else aboard this marvel of a ship, with mahogany wash-basins and paneled walls, plus lovely thick wool taffeta curtains that you could draw in front of your bed at night, creating a snug little private compartment. Chrissie just wished that her father, her brother Jarvie and little nephew, Jarvie Junior, were next door. Their cabin wasn't far away, but in this giant of a ship the labyrinth of corridors was a little daunting. She wished she had a telephone in her cabin so that she could call her father whenever she felt like it. They had private telephones in first-class cabins, it was said.

❧

CAPTAIN TURNER WAS UNEASY ABOUT HIS CREW. THE officers were competent enough, but many of the sea-men were green as grass, some of them only half aware of which way was port and which way starboard. A few of them could barely speak English; many more didn't know their way around the ship. In peacetime he wouldn't have allowed them up the gangway, but now he had to take what he could get. Ever since the war began, the good men had been trickling away. The naval reservists had gone first — fine, experienced sailors every one of them, and impossible to replace now. To make matters worse, every time the ship tied up in New York, a dozen or more hands jumped ship. You could count on it. The worse the war news got, the more hands would be missing when the ship was due to head back to Liverpool. They took their pay and you never saw them again. Young, unmarried men, most of them, just what the army and navy wanted.

Staff Captain John Anderson came in. A burly, amiable man, Anderson was Turner's deputy, with the care and feeding of the passengers' egos his special responsibility. He was good at it, too, a master of the right word at the right time. He took much of the social burden off Turner's shoulders. He knew who mattered and, equally important, who didn't; who had a weakness for alcohol and/or gambling; who could afford to write hefty IOUs and who couldn't. Turner had little patience with such nonsense. He was a sailor, not a maître d'. The less of that social bilge the better.

Not that Turner could escape the bilge altogether. Although Anderson could take over most of the social duties, the hell of the Captain's Table dinner remained to haunt every trip. It was the social high point of the voyage, an event to which, for some ungodly reason, every passenger yearned to be invited. If only they knew how he hated the whole tiresome business! Turner's final choices for guests at his table could gen-erally be categorized as "safe." He had long ago found that he could engage in a reasonably intelligent con-versation with a man who made automobiles, but that he had little in common with artists or philosophers. Alfred Vanderbilt would probably present no difficul-ties at his table, but Charles Frohman and that author man, Hubbard, should probably be avoided. When he shared a meal with some of the richest and most influ-ential people in the world, it amused Turner to think how these same people would have ignored him on land, dressed in a plain blue serge suit instead of his uniform with its gold braid. They would see him as just another provincial with a quaint north-country twang. The funny thing was, on ship, the wealthier they were, the more attentively they listened to his every word. It was as if Admiral Nelson himself sat before them. *How interesting, Captain. What a marvelous grasp of things you have, Captain.* On a couple of occa-sions he had seen women — hefty, broad-beamed spec-imens — actually bend their knees in grotesque curtsies during the introductions before dinner. Did the poor deluded characters really think he was some sort of royalty?

But perhaps it wasn't so fanciful. If only for a few days, he was the supreme authority on this floating kingdom, possessing the power to imprison passengers if they misbehaved, to lead them into disaster if he miscalculated, even to marry them if they insisted, although the legal status of the ceremony was questionable back on dry land.

❧

BY TRADITION THE FIRST DINNER ON ANY VOYAGE tended to be a relatively casual affair. Evening dress was not essential, in recognition of the fact that most passengers had not had time to finish unpacking.

As Margaret Mackworth entered the magnificent dining room with her father, she wondered who their table companions would be. Her trip to New York had been made tedious by a barracuda of a woman from Golders Green, a suburb of northwest London. She had droned on incessantly about her husband, who was something incredibly impor-

Cunard sold souvenir log books so passengers could record their impressions of the trip.

tant at the British embassy in Washington. According to her, Anglo-American relations revolved around her husband; President Wilson ("a moderately pleasant man") never made a decision without first talking it over with him.

This time fate had been kind. Margaret and her father met their table companions: a doctor named Howard Fisher and his sister-in-law, a nurse, Dorothy Conner. Both were on their way to France to start a field hospital. They were a pleasant change from so many saloon passengers, people who appeared to have no interests beyond their families and how well connected they were or their businesses and how profitable they were. Margaret and her father took to the two Americans at once, and before long the four of them were chuckling over the German embassy's advertisement in the morning paper. They all agreed that it was nothing to worry about, a crude attempt to spread alarm and uncertainty.

"But I hope we see *something* exciting," said Dorothy, grinning. "It would be too bad to have to go home and admit that the trip was no more thrilling than going to Coney Island."

A man at the Cunard office had told Howard Fisher that he could rely on the Royal Navy escorting the *Lusitania* when she entered dangerous waters. "They wouldn't allow any enemy ships to get within sight of her," he had declared. "Besides, there's no enemy ship that has the speed to catch up with her. Safe as houses, she is. You can count on it."

The man made it sound as if the mere idea of an enemy attack on the great liner was in slightly bad taste.

❧

THE FLOATING COMMUNITY quickly settled into its routines. There was something about being on board ship that made narrow chests expand, something that made middle-aged men of sedentary habits suddenly feel the urge to stride around the promenade deck sucking in the fresh sea air to cleanse their city-tainted insides, a tonic for the entire system. Sea air sharpened the appetite (as long as the ocean remained reasonably friendly), enabling you to devour enormous quantities of the wickedly tempting meals that flowed from the ship's excellent kitchens: grills and roasts, *bifteck, filet mignon, chapon,* clams and oysters, lobster and crab, eggs that were coddled, eggs that were buttered, eggs that were shirred, eggs that were deviled, bread rolls finger-nipping hot from the ship's bakery, pastries and pancakes, gâteaux and glaces, cheeses named Camembert and Chavignol, Kasseri and Kefalotir. The ship was a veritable cornucopia.

Your enjoyment of things was so much keener on board ship than on dry land. You rediscovered the delights of the tango and the foxtrot. You marveled at

During a prewar crossing, passengers take the air on the ship's boat deck. Named the boat deck because it was where the lifeboats were kept, it was also the largest open area on the ship, which made it a popular place in good weather.

the talent of that fellow Somerset Maugham, although you had thoroughly disapproved of him at home. The ship's concerts, while often offering the finest performers in the world (courtesy of the passenger list), also presented many so-called artistes with far more nerve than talent. Yet in the indulgent, well-fed state generated by shipboard living, you found them highly entertaining. You slept better aboard ship; in fact just settling down snugly wrapped in a deck chair with a good novel often resulted in a nap broken only by the arrival of the steward with a cup of steaming hot broth to keep you going until lunch. And there was no denying how much wittier you became as soon as you were out to sea. Was it the ceaseless wind that stirred the brain cells? Or was it the motion of the sea? Or was it that you finally had the time to apply yourself to the business of amusing your fellow man and woman? Being afloat seemed to add a certain spice to living. No wonder, then, that chance meetings aboard ship tended to assume such signifi-

cance. The lady who might have seemed pleasant enough on a damp day on London's Lower Regent Street could all so easily and rapidly become the love of your life on the boat deck. The moments acquired a certain magic. Only when you stepped ashore did things slot back into their normal places, no matter how hard you tried to cling to the old magic. Seasoned Atlantic travelers knew the feeling well.

∞

ONLY ONE INCIDENT HAD MARRED THE TRIP SO FAR. Soon after departure from New York, an officer came across three young men in a storeroom. They weren't members of the crew, and they weren't passengers. They had no documents, and it was impossible to get more than grunts and gestures from the men. Were they ordinary stowaways? Or potential saboteurs?

Turner ordered the ship searched from end to end. No explosives were found, so if the mysterious trio were saboteurs, they hadn't succeeded in their mission.

(Above) The lifeboats being tested in the harbor. The liner carried enough lifeboats (below) for all on board, but passengers had not been told which boat to go to in an emergency.

THE WAR *at* SEA

WHEN BRITAIN AND Germany went to war in 1914, it was the culmination of more than twenty years of tension between the two nations. It began with the crowning of the irascible Friedrich Wilhelm Viktor Albert as kaiser in 1888. Soon after, he embarked on a program to build up Germany's Imperial Grand Fleet. "Wilhelm's one idea is to have a Navy which shall be larger and stronger than the Royal Navy," his mother told a relative in an indulgent tone, as if discussing her son's latest hobby.

The Anglo-German naval race had begun. Britain won the first round in 1905 with the *Dreadnought*, a heavily armed battleship powered by modern steam turbines similar to those installed in the *Lusitania*. Germany soon responded, building equally powerful vessels, and incorporating better armament and armor plating.

Germany went to war secure in the belief that the British would follow their traditional practice of

K aiser Wilhelm (above) wanted a navy greater than Britain's. (Below) The revolutionary battleship Dreadnought. When war broke out, the British fleet (right) sealed off Germany. To fight back, Tirpitz (above right) turned to his submarines.

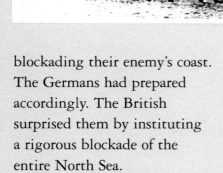

blockading their enemy's coast. The Germans had prepared accordingly. The British surprised them by instituting a rigorous blockade of the entire North Sea.

But if the Germans had miscalculated, so had the British. In response to the blockade, the British expected the German fleet to sally forth in an attempt to break out. A great naval battle would ensue, and the Royal Navy was confident of victory. But the formidable German Admiral Alfred von Tirpitz had other ideas. Britain was an island dependent for its very survival upon enormous amounts of food and raw materials flowing in daily, *by ship*. Shut off the shipping lanes and you defeat Britain. To achieve this Tirpitz turned to his modest force of submarines — a mere twenty, at a time when the Royal Navy

possessed more than seventy. Although Tirpitz had relatively few submarines (or U-boats, from *Unterseeboot*) at his disposal, they were the best in the world, most powered by excellent diesel engines and with a range of some five thousand miles. At a time when the world's navies rated the undersea craft as rather inferior defensive weapons, Tirpitz believed they had great offensive potential. He visualized scores of them in the North Sea, slipping unseen beneath the surface, destroying naval and merchant ships by the dozen, breaking the cruel British blockade, and ultimately winning the war for Germany.

The first few sorties were disappointing; in fact, to Tirpitz's dismay, U-boat losses outnumbered sinkings. But soon he had a stunning victory.

In the early hours of September 22, 1914, a German submarine, the *U-9*, under the command of Lieutenant Otto Weddigen, surfaced off the coast of Belgium. The *U-9* had been on her way to take up station in the Flanders Bight when her compass had failed and she had gone badly off course. The craft was wallowing in choppy seas, so Weddigen had dived to spend the night in calm. As he surfaced, he found that conditions had improved. He found something else: three British cruisers, the *Aboukir*, the *Hogue* and the *Cressy*, sailing in a neat row a few kilometers away. He dived and readied his craft for attack. At 6:20, he fired a torpedo at the *Aboukir*. It blew a massive hole in the cruiser's starboard side, and within minutes, the vessel began to sink. Her captain, John Drummond, thought he had struck a mine. (In September 1914, seamen didn't automatically think of U-boats when sudden explosions occurred at sea.) He signaled to the *Hogue* and the *Cressy* for assistance. Unaware that a U-boat was in the vicinity, both vessels stopped to pick up survivors. Thirty-five minutes after sinking the *Aboukir*, Weddigen fired two torpedoes into the *Hogue*, at a range of

Otto Weddigen (below), commander of the U-9 (left), and his crew (bottom left) opened a new era in warfare. (Right) a freighter falls prey to a U-boat.

300 meters. The cruiser heeled over, mortally wounded. Her crew abandoned her.

Weddigen surfaced briefly to survey the amazing scene. Then he dived again and fired two more torpedoes at the stationary *Cressy*, busily engaged in picking up sailors from the other two cruisers, her captain still believing that mines had been responsible for the disaster. Both of Weddigen's missiles hit their target. The great four-funnel warship rolled slowly to port, her crew scrambling for their lives. For a few horrific minutes, crewmen scurried like tiny insects along

her flat keel, desperately trying to escape. They didn't have much time. The cruiser soon went down, the last of the formation that had steamed so confidently into Weddigen's view little more than an hour before.

It was a signal triumph for Tirpitz's U-boat force. One U-boat had sunk three cruisers, 36,000 tons in all, and had killed 62 RN officers and 1,397 men. Otto Weddigen won the Iron Cross First Class and every member of the crew soon wore the Iron Cross Second Class on his chest.

A month later, the *U-17* sank a British freighter, the *Glitra*. She was the first of countless merchantmen to fall victim to Tirpitz's submarines; but a torpedo didn't sink her. She went down when the U-boat's sailors opened her sea cocks. The German commander had followed the long-established rules of conduct in blockades, firing a shot over the merchantman's bows, boarding her, inspecting her cargo, and permitting the crew to take to the boats before sinking her. Such chivalrous conduct characterized the war's early months. It was short-lived. Early in 1915, with the land war bogged down in the unspeakable misery of the trenches, the Germans declared the waters around the British Isles a war zone. Enemy ships, naval or merchant marine, would be sunk without warning. If neutral vessels chose to enter the war zone they ran the same risks, for the flying of neutral flags by combatants had already become one of the well-established dirty tricks of a battle that knew little mercy.

The underwater crews soon learned their craft. British shipping losses mounted alarmingly. Within a matter of months the U-boat had become the Royal Navy's principal headache; before long the destruction they wrought among British ships would bring Britain close to defeat.

Chapter Four

A Fateful Encounter

O N THURSDAY EVENING, MAY 6, THE *LUSITANIA*'S wireless room received a message from the naval center at Queenstown (now Cobh) on Ireland's south coast warning of submarines in the area. It was the first of four separate warnings. At sunset all outboard lights on the big Cunarder were extinguished and covers were fitted on the skylights. The crew swung out the lifeboats. Thus prepared, the *Lusitania* sailed into the war zone.

The night passed without incident. In the morning passengers awoke to find their ship traveling slowly on a calm sea, surrounded by slowly shifting mountain ranges of mist that extended as far as the eye could see.

The ship's siren wailed a melancholy accompaniment to Oliver Bernard's breakfast. He wished the captain would turn the damned thing off and stop advertising the ship's presence to the Germans. Finishing his meal, Bernard went outside. The air was heavy with moisture; water beaded every window and railing. It looked as if frost had formed on the metal fittings on the davits suspending the lifeboats high over the sea. According to the clock the sun was up, but it couldn't be seen, not even as a glow in the murk. From the deck the siren's mournful dirge seemed subdued, half-hearted. But it was still too noisy, in Bernard's opinion.

The *Lusitania* was near Ireland now, according to a deck officer. "Over there," he said with a grin, stabbing a lean finger over the port side. "If it weren't for

The Lusitania *making speed in peacetime. By 1915, several of her boilers were closed down as an economy measure, so that she was running well below her top speed of twenty-six knots.*

the fog, you'd see it as clear as can be."

Bernard peered into the murk. Were there submarines darting around down there in the fog-shrouded water, like metallic sharks?

❧

THE *U-20* CRUISED SLOWLY ON THE SURFACE, HER CREW enjoying the fresh sea air that crept — hesitantly, it seemed — into the reeking interior while the tiers of wet-cell batteries were being recharged. Four men, including Lieutenant Walther Schwieger, stood guard on the conning tower, watching and listening. It was vital work, for if a destroyer should appear out of the mist, there would be only seconds to dive. U-boat crews had a certain kinship with rabbits; they, too, often had to run for their lives at short notice.

The U-boat had sailed down the west coast of Ireland and around the westerly tip to enter the waters off southern Ireland. The journey had not been without incident. Two days earlier, the frustrated Schwieger had encountered a relic from another age, the 132-ton schooner *Earl of Lathom*. The ancient sailing ship carried no armament that Schwieger could see. She was a poor prize but better than nothing, which was precisely what the *U-20*'s patrol had bagged so far.

Schwieger ordered the U-boat's tanks blown. The submarine thrust her gray flanks above the surface. Clambering up the narrow ladder to the conning tower, Schwieger commanded the *Earl of Lathom* to heave to. The skipper of the schooner obeyed. He had little choice. Schwieger sent a boarding party to examine the ship. Sure enough, she was British. After ordering the five-man crew to take to their rickety lifeboat, Schwieger opened fire with his deck gun. The shots tore through the schooner's old timbers. Staggering, cringing as if in pain, the ancient vessel took her punishment and, after a dozen shots, she quietly slipped beneath the sea.

Later that day Schwieger spotted a 3,000-ton steamer emerging from a fog bank. Although the steamer displayed conspicuous signs testifying to her neutral status, Schwieger was suspicious. He suspected

the British were up to their usual dirty tricks. Quickly he made up his mind and fired a torpedo at the steamer. It missed. The steamer headed away into the mist.

Schwieger swore. Nearly a week on patrol and all he had achieved was the littering of the ocean with a few kilograms of firewood. When would his luck turn?

It happened in the early hours of the following morning. A 5,858-ton merchantman, the *Candidate*, appeared. Schwieger deemed this ship safe enough to attack on the surface, but he decided against giving her any warning. Those packing cases on the deck could conceal 4.7-inch guns. In fact, knowing the British, they almost certainly did.

The U-boat's gun crew quickly prepared their weapon. Schwieger gave the order to fire. The submarine trembled, recoiling as the first shots rang out. Direct hits. One after the other. In a matter of minutes the ship was wallowing helplessly. The crew lowered the four lifeboats and rowed for their lives. Their ship had acquired a heavy list, but still she floated. Schwieger fired one of his torpedoes. It ripped through the hull by the engine room. At once the ship began to settle, and Schwieger finished her off with gunfire. At last something worth recording in his log!

An hour later he spotted a large passenger steamer. The vessel flew no colors, but both Schwieger and Lanz agreed that it was British, probably a White Star liner. About 14,000 tons, Lanz estimated. Schwieger attempted to maneuver his craft for a torpedo attack. He calculated it all to a nicety. But a lookout on the steamer spotted the U-boat. In a few minutes the ship had vanished into the mist, leaving the U-boat far behind. For the benefit of the crew, Schwieger shrugged philosophically. There were plenty of other targets waiting to be found.

A couple of hours later the *U-20* came across a medium-sized merchantman. The ship flew no flag and neither he nor Lanz could identify her, but no neutral ship would ply these waters without a prominent flag. She was British; Schwieger would bet a month's pay on

Gun crews hidden behind hay bales fire on an unsuspecting U-boat. The British had taken to arming
merchant ships and were even creating heavily armed decoy vessels, called Q-ships, meant to lure U-boats into battle.
As a result, submarine commanders were wary of attacking their prey while surfaced.

U nder the traditional rules of war, a submarine attacked unarmed ships on the surface, after first warning its victim and allowing the crew to escape.

it. Lanz agreed. Approaching unseen, he fired a single torpedo. It worked perfectly, striking the merchant-man close to her foremast. The ship quivered, her bow dipping as if in surrender. Her crew took to their boats and rowed away. Schwieger let them escape before he put a second torpedo into her. The ship went down within minutes. Invariably such moments of triumph were seasoned with sadness; no true sailor enjoyed the sight of a ship in her death throes. Lanz checked his reference books and found that their latest victim was the 5,495-ton *Centurion* of the Harrison line.

Schwieger's mood improved. At last the patrol was showing results! But should he go on to the waters off Liverpool, as ordered? He had a feeling he might do better to remain in this area. He had already used three torpedoes. His instructions were to save two "tin fish" for the journey home.

Perhaps, with a bit of luck, he would come across a really important target.

❧

THE FOG BEGAN TO THIN. NOW IT WAS LIKE A gossamer curtain between the ship and the land, reminding Julia Sullivan of special effects she had seen in Broadway shows.

Yes, that uncertain line on the horizon was definitely land. The first sight of it seemed to send a thrill through the passengers lining the ship's port side. No matter how many times you crossed the ocean, the first sight of land was exciting, a sort of affirmation that the world had managed to get along despite your absence on the high seas.

Standing at the rail, Julia watched the hazy coastline and wondered how she would take to living on a farm after the years in New York. She and Flor had changed a lot. You couldn't see as much of the world as they had without it having an effect. The question was, how would they strike the locals? There was a very real danger, Flor had remarked, of putting people's backs up by talking too much of the wonders of life "over there" in America. Answer their questions, he said, and leave it at that. He was right, of course. But did he really think they could pick up the farm and make a go of it? Were all the brave words for his benefit as much as hers?

She tried to distinguish landmarks in the distance. Was that Cape Clear? Funny, when she left home her heart ached for Ireland; now she was seeing Ireland again and her heart ached for America.

❧

CHRISSIE AITKEN WATCHED LITTLE JARVIE KICK THE football the sailors had given him. They had made it out of paper, tying the pieces into a ball that looked solid enough, but didn't go very far. With any luck it would survive until Liverpool.

Her father's health seemed to have improved. The sea air and the nearness of Scotland had put color in his cheeks and a spring in his step. He spent every day telling Jarvie Junior about all the wonderful things they would soon be doing together.

❧

CAPTAIN TURNER HAD BEEN UP SINCE DAWN. IT WAS the last day of the voyage, and in his experience twenty-four hours was never long enough for such days. Departures were hectic, but arrivals seemed to breed unexpected problems by the dozen. Turner was now sailing at eighteen knots, partly because of the fog that still dotted the sea in untidy little patches, but principally because he planned to sail straight through to Liverpool. He wanted to arrive with the tide in the early hours of Saturday morning and head straight into harbor without stopping to pick up a pilot. He had worked it all out in his meticulous way, down to the last detail.

❧

THE ADMIRALTY HADN'T TOLD TURNER THAT SINCE HE had set off from New York, a total of twenty-three ships had been sunk by U-boats in the waters around the British Isles. The navy was worried that this might be the beginning of a major new U-boat campaign. Concern was growing for the safety of several ships, most notably the *Lusitania*. Had Winston Churchill, the First Sea Lord, been at the Admiralty, he might have diverted naval units to escort the mighty Cunarder and other merchant ships to their destinations. But Churchill was in France visiting Sir John French, commander of the British Expeditionary Force. Rumor had it that he was angling to be relieved of the Admiralty and given a top military command.

In Queenstown Vice-Admiral Coke listened to the reports of U-boat activity. It seemed to him that the *Lusitania* was sailing directly into an area of extreme danger. But Coke had neither the authority nor the means to help the big Cunarder. His modest force of obsolete patrol vessels, contemptuously called "the Gilbert and Sullivan Navy" by the rest of the fleet, was too small, too slow and too old. None of his ships had the *Lusitania*'s speed, so how could they protect her from anything? Besides, if by some miracle his destroyers did manage to form an escort, the liner would, legally speaking, become part of a naval unit and a legitimate target for attack without warning by U-boats.

Frustrated, Coke scowled out of his office window at the fog. It was definitely thinning. According to the weather experts, the sun would soon burn it all away. A fine afternoon was in store.

❧

FOR THE CREW OF *U-20*, FRIDAY MORNING HAD BEEN tense, with the mist wreathing about the sea, odd little clusters of white, hard on visibility and the nerves. Schwieger had spent the past few hours furtively slinking along the surface looking for trouble. He was thankful that he found none. Now conditions seemed to be improving. The batteries were almost charged. Soon he could go back on the offensive.

The blurred outline of a naval vessel appeared through the mist, heading straight for the U-boat. Trouble! He dived quickly. Soon afterward, a ship passed directly over the U-boat, the din of its engine reverberating through the submarine's steel hull. Using his periscope, Schwieger spotted the ship, an elderly cruiser. A fine target. He attempted to give chase, but it was hopeless. The cruiser (later identified as the *Juno*, built in 1898, one of Admiral Coke's company of ancient vessels) headed away toward Queenstown.

The crew relaxed. The crisis was over, for the moment.

❧

VICE-ADMIRAL COKE SENT A ONE-WORD MESSAGE TO the *Lusitania*: QUESTOR. The Cunarder responded promptly: WESTRONA. In the coded exchange Queenstown asked what M.V. (Merchant Vessel) Code the ship held; the response was the first edition of the M.V. Code.

Captain Turner wondered if he was about to be ordered to put into Queenstown. It had happened a few months before when he was in command of the *Transylvania*. The unscheduled call had caused a lot of irritation among the passengers, many of whom complained about important business appointments and relatives arriving on trains in Liverpool to meet the ship. "It's by order of the Admiralty," Turner had told the complainers. "War emergency instructions."

On that occasion his ship had been carrying important cargo: heavy guns made in America for use on British warships.

But he received no such order on May 7, 1915.

Sunshine began to sparkle on the sea. Turner doubled his lookouts and ordered closed any watertight doors that wouldn't interfere with the ship's operation. But at the same time passengers were opening portholes, taking advantage of the fine spring weather. No one told them not to.

Turner sailed on into the waters near Queenstown,

Robert Leith, one of the Lusitania's *wireless officers. He may have taken Vice-Admiral Coke's message from Queenstown.*

———◦◦◦———

much as he had done dozens of times before. Although he would later deny it, he made no attempt to follow any of the instructions issued by the Admiralty for the benefit of merchant skippers in this area that had seen so many U-boats. He steamed along close to Brow Head, Galley Head and the Old Head of Kinsale despite the Admiralty's instructions to merchant ships to stay away from headlands where U-boats tended to lurk, waiting for prey. The Admiralty also ordered merchantmen to sail in the middle of the sea lane, which in that area meant about seventy miles offshore. At the time the *Lusitania* was about a dozen miles from the Irish coast. Moreover, skippers were instructed to sail at top speed near harbors; the *Lusitania* was making about eighteen knots as she neared Queenstown. Finally, the Admiralty recommended that merchantmen steer a zigzag course. Turner's course was undeviating.

Turner didn't argue with the reasoning of the bureaucrats at the Admiralty. Everything they said made sense. And no doubt most captains of warships were enthusiastic zigzaggers. But they didn't have to worry about the cost of coal or the comfort of passengers. Customers who had forked out more for a five-day journey from New York to Liverpool than most people earned in a year did not take kindly to being tossed around in their cabins while their ship made pretty patterns all over the ocean. They had paid for a smooth, luxurious trip. It was Turner's responsibility to see that they got it.

A lthough they were more vulnerable on the surface, U-boats were much faster and had better visibility there than underwater. Once lookouts had spotted a target, the submarine could attack on the surface, or if its opponent were dangerous, while submerged.

THE DAILY POSTING OF THE SHIP'S PROGRESS RAISED A few eyebrows. In twenty-four hours they had sailed only 462 miles, a shade over nineteen miles per hour. Passengers who studied the bulletin agreed that it was undoubtedly the fog that had slowed them down.

✌

DECKHAND LESLIE MORTON CAME ON DUTY AT NOON. In a little while he would be sent forward to take up his duties as an extra lookout on the starboard bow. For the moment, however, he had to work in the baggage room manhandling the great steamer trunks, some of them weighing a hundred pounds or more, getting them organized for the arrival in Liverpool. Most of Leslie's fellow deckhands were working down there, sweating buckets as they dragged the heavy trunks out of their corners, checked them against the all-important master list (the Old Testament, one hand called it) and then wheeled them out to the elevator to be whisked off to the upper decks.

Leslie and his brother, John, had sailed to America on board an old sailing ship, the *Naiad*, bound for Australia. After a few days in New York, they decided to jump ship and go home. Their original intention had been to travel back to Britain as passengers aboard the *Lusitania*, but to their delight they had found that the big Cunarder was short of deckhands. The two Mortons lost no time in signing on. They found the work hard and they made plenty of mistakes, frequently getting lost in the maze of corridors and confusing the names of the various departments and, worse, the officers in charge. But all in all it was a good experience; the *Lusitania* was a fine ship and most of the crew were friendly fellows when you got to know them. Already the Morton brothers were talking about signing on for another run. They wanted to be able to tell people that they worked on the *Lusitania*. Hers was a name to reckon with.

✌

THE *U-20* SURFACED AT 12:45 P.M. SCHWIEGER CLAMbered up to the conning tower and jotted down his observations for later transfer to the ship's log. Condi-

tions had improved, he noted. Visibility was excellent; the last traces of morning fog had disappeared. The sea was uncommonly calm, like an enormous pond. Too bad he had to spend his time looking for ships to attack; it was a perfect afternoon for relaxing on the beach, enjoying the weather and some attractive company and discussing life and art and sharing a bottle of wine.

Unfortunately there were more pressing matters to be considered. The morale of the crew, for instance. One or two of them were definitely suffering from strain. Schwieger knew the signs: the slightly metallic quality to the voice, the furtive, hunted look in the eyes. They were good men, every one of them but, like everyone, they had their limits. Thank God it would soon be time to set course for home.

The Irish coast was a thin dark line on the horizon.

Schwieger munched on his lunch of bread and sausage. It tasted and stank of diesel fuel. How long, he wondered, before one's insides became plugged up with the filthy stuff?

His eyes narrowed. A smudge of smoke. Six or seven miles away, he estimated. Automatically, he checked the time: 13:20.

He waited. The smoke gave way to funnels. Four of them.

His excitement mounted. Only the biggest, most important ships sported four funnels. This one was steaming along parallel to the coast. Schwieger quickly calculated the tracks and estimated the speeds of the two vessels.

"Prepare to dive!"

✌

MARGARET MACKWORTH AND HER FATHER SIPPED THEIR coffee, feeling pleasantly full. This time tomorrow they would be back home in Wales, and it was just as well. The meals were simply too good on the *Lusitania*. A few more and the evidence of them would become all too apparent.

Howard Fisher and Dorothy Conner had already gone to their cabins to start packing. The voyage was almost over, Margaret mused, and now the real world

with all its problems was about to intrude
once more. She realized with a little pang
of guilt that she had hardly given her husband a thought since leaving New York.
She still didn't know what she should do
about him. Perhaps nothing. Keep on playing the game of make-believe. Keep pre-
tending that all was well. That was the way
untold numbers of so-called marriages were
maintained year after year. Sometimes such
marriages worked themselves out. Why not
hers?

Margaret apologized to her father. He
had been saying something — something
amusing, to judge by his smile — and she hadn't heard
a word.

LESLIE MORTON TOOK HIS POSITION ON THE STARBOARD
bow. He exchanged a few words with his predecessor.
Everything was quiet.

It was strange, how calm the sea was. Almost eerie.

*he Lusitania off
Ireland on a
westward trip (above).
Typically, she sailed as
close to land on the homeward leg of the voyage.
Although he had been warned to stay out from
land once in the war zone
off the British Isles (inset
below), Turner kept to the
coastal waters where
U-boats lay in wait as
shown (below).*

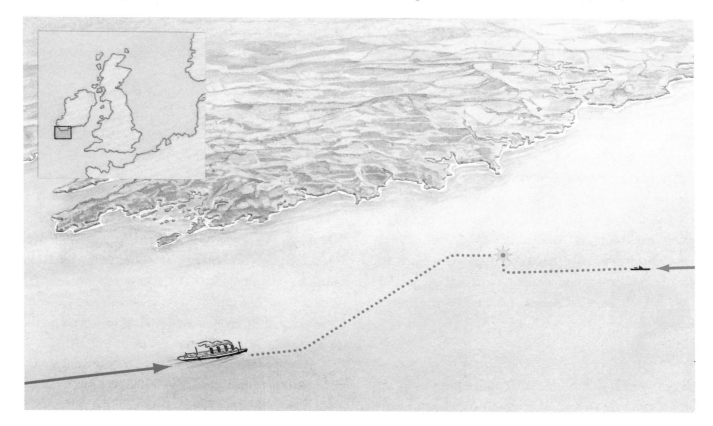

The ship hardly swayed as she sliced her way through the water. According to the men who'd served on her for years, this had been one of the easiest trips ever. Leslie and his brother didn't know how lucky they were, they said. As usual such comments led to breathless reminiscences of the storms they'd weathered. Waves that made matchwood of lifeboats. Passengers who slithered helplessly across first-class lounge floors, only to be run down by grand pianos that had broken free of their restraints. Crewmen lost at sea: "One moment he was there, large as life. Next he'd gone. And he owed me sixpence..." Some of the crew had been on the *Lusitania* when she encountered that monster of a storm in January 1910. A wave at least eighty feet high hit the ship with such devastating force that it shoved the entire bridge aft several inches. The impact tore the wheel from its pedestal and flooded the enclosed bridge to a depth of five feet.

The old salts never talked about the enjoyable trips. It was the desperate struggles for survival, the no-holds-barred fights with the elements that they remembered. They loved to try to scare newcomers with such stories. And, Leslie had to admit, they usually succeeded.

He studied the ocean section by section, from left to right, then back again, as he had been taught. The trouble was, the process could be almost hypnotic. You had to keep your wits about you or you'd drop off. Let that happen and you'd find yourself in irons down in the bilge.

SCHWIEGER ESTIMATED THE BIG SHIP'S SPEED AT TWENTY knots. He bit his lip in irritation. It looked as if she

would escape him. With his electric motors providing a top speed of only nine knots, the *U-20* wouldn't be able to converge with the steamer's track in time. That was the inescapable truth. The prize would elude him.

Or would it?

Incredibly, the liner was turning to starboard by

A U-boat officer searches for targets using the ship's periscope. With the submarine's relatively low underwater speed, a U-boat commander could only hope that his target didn't get away before he could fire a torpedo.

some thirty degrees. Schwieger sent a brief message of thanks to the Almighty. The big ship was diligently placing herself in just the right position to be attacked. The heat and the stench were forgotten as his quarry approached. In his mind's eyes he could see the converging lines — the *U-20*'s, the liner's — meeting just about *there*.

The crew's eyes were on him, staring, bloodshot, set deep in grubby, unshaven faces. Awaiting his command.

STRIKING FROM BENEATH THE WAVES

O nce a target was spotted, the U-boat's control room (right) came alive. But firing meant more than just a command to the torpedo room (below). The U-boat had to maneuver into firing position, allowing for the speed of the target and its angle relative to the submarine. If all went well, the torpedo's motor (1)

started, driven by compressed air (2), the propellers (3) began to turn, and the safety protecting the detonator began to unwind (4), arming the 300-pound warhead (5).

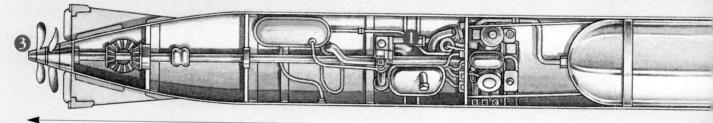

17'

FELIX
SCHWORMSTÄDT
1915

According to Lanz, the big liner was the *Maure-tania* or the *Lusitania*. The British were using liners as so-called auxiliary cruisers and as troop ships.

More than thirty thousand tons...

The crew reported the U-boat ready for attack. The atmosphere in the narrow hull became electric. It was as if a button had been pressed, charging the air, tightening every nerve. Eyes glued to the periscope sight, Schwieger called out the adjustments he wanted made to the torpedo as hunter and hunted drew closer. The wheelman reported the adjustments made. The torpedo was ready for firing.

Schwieger prayed that the big ship didn't change course again. If she turned to port, toward the coast, he would lose the biggest prize of his life.

Seven hundred and fifty meters...600...550...

Five hundred.

Still the ship didn't stray from her path.

Schwieger's fingers gripped the periscope.

"Fire!"

A hiss and a shudder.

The torpedo thrust its phosphor-bronze snout into the chilly water under the control of the assembly of balances, pendulums, gyros and motors in its belly.

Everything worked, for a change. A compressed-air motor thrust the torpedo forward at a brisk twenty-two knots. Twin propellers rotated in opposite directions, keeping the missile steady, countering any tendency for it to twist and stray from course.

The rushing water spun a small propeller mounted on the torpedo's nose. It fitted over the trigger, which on impact would slam back into the torpedo's warhead, setting off the fulminate-of-mercury charge and, instantaneously, the cellulose-nitrate primer and the main charge, 300 pounds of a form of TNT known as trotyl.

Turning along a threaded rod like some harmless child's toy, the propeller soon reached the end of the rod and fell away, still turning.

The torpedo had armed itself.

Chapter Five

Abandon Ship!

D ECKHAND LESLIE MORTON SPOTTED A BURST of bubbles some five hundred yards away on the starboard side. A moment later his wide eyes caught sight of an unusual sight. Something was streaking along just beneath the surface...heading straight for the *Lusitania*. For an instant his brain seemed paralyzed. Then comprehension hit him like a sharp blow.

He swung around and, using the megaphone they had given him, yelled to the bridge.

"Torpedoes coming on the starboard side!"

He saw what he thought were a pair of trails and took them to be two torpedoes. In fact what he probably saw was the actual trail of the torpedo about ten feet down and a secondary trail created by bubbles as they broke the surface. Another man might have repeated the electrifying announcement until someone on the bridge acknowledged it, but Leslie's orders were straightforward. Report any sighting, then resume your watch. Besides, a chilling thought had just struck him. His brother John was off duty below, probably fast asleep in his bunk. He had to get down there, to warn him.

Leslie left his post.

Thirty irreplaceable seconds ticked away before another member of the crew spotted the oncoming torpedo. Thomas Quinn, the starboard lookout in the crow's nest, saw the deadly trail from his vantage point more than a hundred feet above the deck. His warning alerted the officers on the bridge.

It was too late. The *Lusitania*'s fate was sealed.

MARGARET MACKWORTH AND HER FATHER STROLLED out of the dining room and made their way toward the elevator. The Old Head of Kinsale could be seen in the distance, a small promontory thrusting out into the sun-dappled sea. Beyond was Queenstown. Only a few hours more and the *Lusitania* would be pulling into Liverpool.

A dull thud, more felt than heard, interrupted Margaret's thoughts. For a moment she wondered if she had imagined it.

Several decks higher up, Oliver Bernard heard a much louder bang. He had been standing near the verandah café looking out over the water when the luminescent trail caught his attention. For a stupid, unthinking moment its significance didn't register. Then, with a jolt, he understood.

Bernard gazed, transfixed, until the trail disappeared from view at his feet; it seemed to be thrusting its way into the very heart of the ship.

He closed his eyes and tightened his grip on the railing. The moment passed. Nothing happened. The torpedo must have missed. Then the ship seemed to recoil as a sharp, stinging bang reverberated through her. The wooden rail shivered in Bernard's grasp.

Well, that wasn't too bad, he thought. A moment later came the second explosion.

❧

TO CHRISSIE AITKEN, BUSY IN HER CABIN, THE SOUND of the torpedo's impact was just a bit of a thud, hardly worth a mention.

A few moments after the initial explosion, the Lusitania *was rocked by a far more powerful secondary explosion, which threw debris and water high into the air.*

But to Julia Sullivan, standing at the rail on the second-cabin promenade deck on the port side of the ship, it was "the most dreadful explosion the world has ever heard." She had been studying the Irish coast through binoculars that her husband had borrowed from a member of the crew. Startled by the explosion, she dropped them. Something cracked when they hit the deck.

It felt as if the ship had tripped over some giant's foot in the ocean. Julia had to grab Flor's sleeve to steady herself. She stooped to retrieve the binoculars.

"Don't worry about those things," Flor said.

❧

TO CAPTAIN TURNER THE IMPACT OF THE TORPEDO sounded like the banging of a door on a windy day.

❧

SOME PASSENGERS NEVER DID HEAR THE FIRST EXPLOsion. But all heard the second. Almost everyone thought another torpedo had hit the ship. Many thought the second explosion was far more powerful than the first. Some later claimed that the two explosions had totally different sounds. Others noticed little difference. It all depended where you happened to be at that moment.

Oliver Bernard hadn't moved since the first bang. The second sent him toppling backward. He threw up his hands, instinctively trying to protect himself from the great eruption of water, smoke and dirt that sprang up before him. It all hung there for a weirdly extended moment, "a white mountain" that abruptly dissolved and came crashing down — chunks of wood, fragments of bent metal, torn bits of tarpaulin, all spinning and tumbling, then pattering and bouncing on the deck beside him.

"What the deuce!"

The man beside him sounded offended. Bernard would not have been surprised to hear him say that he intended to lodge a severe complaint about the incident.

As if staggering under the weight of the debris, the huge liner began to pitch to starboard.

LIEUTENANT SCHWIEGER STARED IN DISBELIEF. NOT only had his torpedo found its mark, but its effect had been devastating. Schwieger had half expected the vessel to go on her way, shrugging off the effect of the hit the way an elephant might shrug off a bee sting. But this ship was already settling, her bow well down.

Later Schwieger recorded in his war diary that he observed "great confusion" on board the Cunarder. It looked to him as if the ship was going to capsize. He thought only briefly of sending another torpedo into her, noting that it would have been "impossible" for him to fire a second torpedo at "this crowd of people struggling to save their lives."

❧

SOME PASSENGERS AND CREW HAD NO DOUBT FROM THE start that the Lusitania was doomed. Others thought the ship had survived the two explosions without serious damage. The smoke cleared away. The ship kept sailing. People stood on deck much as they had been doing all week, looking out over the ocean, unwilling to believe that anything could be seriously amiss.

In her cabin, Chrissie Aitken wondered if she was getting sick; something was happening to her sense of balance. Then she heard a steward in the corridor knocking on cabin doors, asking everyone to go up on deck at once. Please. She went to the door.

"Up top, miss."

"What's wrong?"

"Hurry. Get up on deck. Don't worry about your things. Just get up on deck. Quick!"

Chrissie started to ask him why, but he had already gone. She could hear him scurrying along, rapping in a rhythmic way on every door, his Cockney accent sounding almost comical as he told his passengers to get up on deck.

Chrissie paused for a moment, wishing her father was there. Where was he? And her brother and Jarvie Junior? Did they know what had happened? Did they have their life belts?

She had to find the others. Heaven knows what they might do if they didn't have her there to keep an eye on them. She went out into the corridor and followed a great stream of passengers up a wide staircase that seemed oddly off balance.

The moment Chrissie got on deck, she realized why. The ship had taken on a strange angle, as if a strong wind was blowing it over. But there was no wind. The sun beamed down. It was a delightful day, bright and hot. And, as if bent on enjoying it, people swarmed up onto the deck, chattering, glancing in every direction.

But their faces reflected uncertainty and, in a few cases, outright terror. She couldn't see her father or the others.

A sailor with a raspy voice snapped, "Where's your life jacket, miss?"

With a shock she realized that she had been concerned about the others' life jackets but she hadn't thought of hers.

"I don't have one," she said. "I'm really sorry."

"Take mine," he ordered. "Here, I'll help you get

*A*fter the ship was hit, there was confusion about the nature of the two explosions. Although most agreed that a torpedo had hit forward, near or under the bridge (right), some people were convinced that a second torpedo had hit the ship farther aft, between the third and fourth funnels (above), with far more devastating results.

it on." He pointed at a lifeboat. "Then get on that. Don't muck about. Do it *now*!"

※

MARGARET MACKWORTH FELT THE DECK SHUDDER beneath her feet. For an instant all was deathly quiet. Then a burble of high-pitched chatter echoed through the ship. Margaret glanced at her father. They were about to enter the elevator. Instinctively both stepped back. The action undoubtedly saved their lives.

Margaret's father glanced up and down the corridor, frowning. He told her to go to her cabin to get her life belt. He would get his.

"We'll meet on the boat deck," he said.

As she ran down the stairs, Margaret found that she had to support herself with the railing. The world had begun to tilt. And it had gone dark, although there was enough natural light filtering in from outside to see where you were going. Nevertheless, an elderly man

slipped and fell on the stairs. Margaret helped him to his feet. He thanked her and went on his way, mumbling to no one in particular. Sharp-smelling smoke had begun to wreathe odd little patterns in the air. Margaret wondered why she wasn't more frightened.

Her cabin was on B-deck, at the end of a short passage. As she hurried, the ship lurched. She stumbled and collided with a stewardess coming the other way. Absurdly, the two wasted precious moments apologizing to each other.

Margaret collected her life belt from her cabin. With a final glance at her bed, on which she had laid out all the new clothes she had purchased at Saks and Lord and Taylor, she went back into the corridor and headed for her father's cabin. She had an idea that she might find him sorting through his precious papers. He wasn't there, although his life belt was. She took it, scribbled a note to him and placed it on his dressing

DEATH THROES OF A LEVIATHAN

Within five minutes of the torpedoing, the Lusitania was doomed. Already listing badly to starboard, the ship was literally plowing its way deeper into the water, pushed on by its powerful turbines.

1 *Outside the grand entrance on the boat deck, a large crowd gathered. No lifeboat drills had been held for passengers during the crossing, and uncertain what to do, they milled about waiting for instructions.*

2 *On the starboard side, the number one and number three boats were being lowered. The number five boat had disappeared — blown off its davits by the explosion.*

3 *One of the few signs of damage topside was a lid missing from one of the Lusitania's forward ventilators. It had been blown off by the powerful second explosion.*

4 *In those first few minutes, another large group of passengers from deep within the ship had poured onto the top deck of the second-class deckhouse.*

5 *Still at his post on the Lusitania's wing bridge, Captain Turner attempted to maneuver the ship toward the Irish coast, in the hope of beaching her.*

table. She waited for an anxious moment while the babble of voices and clatter of footsteps intruded in odd little explosions of sound. Where *was* he? Had he fallen on the stairs like the man she saw? Maybe he was lying in a corner at that moment, unable to move. Or perhaps he had somehow found another life belt and had already gone up to the deck as they had arranged. Yes, that had to be it.

The corridor outside the cabin was empty, a small oasis of calm. But a few steps brought her to the main corridor where a solid mass of people went streaming by, heading for the companionway. Some looked alarmed, others merely puzzled, as if they had just awakened. Margaret hurried up the stairs into the sunlight and onto the sloping deck. She immediately caught sight of Howard Fisher and Dorothy Conner. Sailors were hard at work preparing to lower one of the lifeboats.

"Everything's going to be all right," said Howard. The women nodded automatically, as if they believed him.

They stood with their legs braced against the deck's angle. From somewhere deep within the ship came the sound of metal twisting and bending, screeching like a tormented animal.

"Well, I wanted some excitement." Dorothy managed a shaky smile.

Farther forward a scrambling mob of passengers came streaming up from the *Lusitania*'s pitch-black innards, wide-eyed and terrified. Their voices harsh with panic, they hurled themselves at the lifeboat being readied for launching. There was no order, just an elemental struggle for survival. Men pushed ahead of women to get into the boat. They ignored a ship's officer who was trying to restore order.

Dismayed, Margaret remarked to Dorothy, "I always thought a shipwreck was a well-organized affair."

"So did I," Dorothy replied, "but I've learned a lot in the last five minutes."

Screams pierced the air like high-pitched shots.

SUPPLEMENT TO THE SPHERE, MAY 15, 1915]

No. 8.—THE DOOMED "LUSIT

IRISH COAST- Cork County

STERN BRIDGE

2nd Class Quarters

Palm Lounge

his stylized period illustration shows the Lusitania *going down on a fairly even keel as Irish fishermen race to the rescue. In fact, the launch of the lifeboats was considerably more chaotic than shown here.*

94

[SUPPLEMENT TO THE SPHERE, MAY 15, 1915

iv—v

A" : How the Irish Rescuers Hurried to the Scene of the Tragedy.

CORK

QUEENSTOWN
from which
assistance was
despatched

KINSALE
First Boats despatched

Roches Point
entrance to
Cork Harbour

Daunt's
Rock

Lighthouse on
Old Head of Kinsale
Keeper telephones
to Kinsale

Position
of 1ᵗ Class
Dining
Saloon

Wireless
Cabin

Distance from Liner
to Headland, 8 miles

Trawlers which
rendered assistance

Captains
Bridge

Bow becoming
submerged

DRAWN BY D. MACPHERSON WITH THE ASSISTANCE OF SURVIVORS. MAY, 1915

The sharply increasing list of the ship had tipped a lifeboat during lowering. Passengers tumbled into the water, shrieking and struggling, their lifeboat crashing down among them.

Appalled, Margaret turned away. She made no attempt to get into a boat. Was she waiting for some officer to come and shepherd first-class passengers to their appointed places? She didn't know. Her neatly organized world had disintegrated around her. Obviously many other passengers were similarly infected by a numbing sense of unreality. They seemed to be moving around the deck like a swarm of bees who did not

The Lusitania's rapidly growing list to starboard and the crew's inexperience hampered attempts to launch the boats. On the port side, boats had to slide down the side of the ship; on the starboard side, several boats tipped on launching.

know where the queen had gone.

Still there was no sign of her father. All around her bobbed hundreds of faces, all unfamiliar, some frightened, some looking around like spectators at a sports event, anxious not to miss anything that was going on, but apparently believing that none of it had any direct influence on their well-being. A man was having difficulty lighting a cigarette. His match kept going out, and for some reason he seemed to find this amusing. People were moving in a strangely jerky fashion, like characters in a motion-picture show.

Howard suddenly realized that he and Dorothy didn't have life belts. He hurried off, promising to return in a few minutes.

The moment he disappeared down the steps, the ship shifted, partially righting herself. It was as if Howard's movements had been enough to tilt the vast ship back to normal, Margaret thought, and then she chided herself for letting such ridiculous thoughts enter her mind when a ship was sinking beneath her and her father was missing.

"She's righting herself...I told you. Everything's going to be hunky-dory," someone said, sounding as if he was trying to convince himself as much as the people around him. Another man explained in an oddly leisurely manner that the ship's renowned safety features were now correcting the situation. The bulkheads had been closed. Soon everything would be back to normal.

Then the whole structure shifted again, like an immense creature that had been disturbed in its sleep. Groaning, squealing, creaking, the ship seemed about to turn right over. Margaret clutched a railing for support. She wondered if these sights were the last she would ever see. She thought of her husband. He had no idea all this was happening, none at all. It was quite incredible.

Thuds and bangs reverberated beneath her feet. The great ship had lost her old feeling of solidity. Steam and smoke vomited out of her, showering the decks with soot.

An officer bellowed through cupped hands, "The captain asks everyone to keep calm. Don't worry. Everything will be all right."

"Is he kidding?" Dorothy remarked, again managing a brave smile.

Howard returned, drenched, his normally immaculate hair dark and wet, pasted across his forehead, his collar wrenched open, his silk necktie awry. He had to pull himself up the steps by the handrail.

"Can't trust those lifeboats," he said. "We'll have to jump." He might have been telling them that they had to have dinner in the verandah café because the dining room was full. He handed a life belt to Dorothy and said he'd had to wade through deep water to get the belts from their cabins.

"Did you see my father?" Margaret asked.

"Sorry."

Margaret bit her lip. Where was he? Why hadn't he come to the deck, as he'd promised? Despair seemed to grow like a sickness inside her.

She looked over the side. The water was only a few feet away now. Passengers were standing on the edge of the deck, as if preparing to step into a swimming pool. Around the ship, heads bobbed in the water and clutching hands reached for help.

Old fears of water tightened around Margaret's throat like icy fingers, but she fought them off. *Must think. Must be sensible.*

I'd better unhook my skirt, she thought as the deck's angle increased. *Can't swim with it on, can I?* At the same instant she admitted to herself that she couldn't swim much with it off, either.

"We have to..." Howard begged.

"I know, but..."

And then there was no time left. The sea came reaching for them, splashing over hatches and ventilators, around now-empty davits and truncated stretches of railing, greedily taking possession of the dying hulk.

⚓

AVIS DOLPHIN HAD BEEN HAVING LUNCH WITH HER friends Hilda Ellis and Sarah Smith when the torpedo hit. A dull thud startled the diners. The room seemed to shake itself like a dog coming out of the water. Forks paused midway to mouths. People glanced at one another. What was going on?

The second explosion came as if in answer to the question. It had a totally different sound and it seemed to burst from the very heart of the ship. Plates and glasses slid off the tables. A waiter went sprawling, his tray and its contents crashing among seated diners.

"Torpedo!"

The word struck fear into Avis's heart. She had heard the talk among the passengers. About submarines. About torpedoes. But hadn't they also said that no submarine in the world could catch the *Lusitania*? They had all sounded so confident that she hadn't given the problem another thought.

Suddenly most of the neatly seated diners sprang to their feet. They swarmed toward the door, confused, frightened. Avis lost sight of Hilda, who had been sitting beside her.

"Come on, Avis. Grab my hand. Now!"

Startled, Avis looked up to see Mr. Holbourn, the tweedy Scotsman. He was still chewing and he looked untroubled, as if he intended to go back and finish his lunch when this was over. Calmly holding her hand, he held her back from the frantic press trying to squeeze through the dining-room doors.

Once the way was clear, Holbourn took Avis in tow, with Hilda and Sarah trailing behind. The deck tilted. From one side came a scream, then a shouted order.

In the cabin, Holbourn took the life belts from their rack and helped Avis into hers, mumbling the instructions to himself as he read them. He made the belt snug around Avis's waist and shoulders.

"No need to be frightened," he said in his reassuring way. "I'm sure everything will be all right. But better safe than sorry. We'll go up on the deck. I expect we'll be back again in a little while..."

He flashed a quick grin as he took Avis's hand again. "Let's go up on deck. I do like to be able to see what's happening, don't you?"

The four of them hurried out of the cabin and up the stairs. They had almost reached the top of the companionway when the lights went out.

Captain Turner had ordered the ship turned to port, toward the coast that looked so close, sparkling in the spring sunshine. Slowly the bow had begun to edge around a degree or two.

At that moment the ship's electrical and hydraulic power died.

For the passengers deep in the bowels of the ship, the loss of power was catastrophic. They were blinded. The familiar corridors and companionways suddenly became obstacle courses. Where someone lit a match, the thrusting horde stepped on each other's feet as they strained to keep the flickering flame in sight. Where there were no matches or flashlights, there was no alternative but to struggle on in the darkness, thumping into unseen obstacles.

The first-class elevators that had been the source of such pride had become death traps. Those inside couldn't get out; those on the outside couldn't get in to help them.

Equally powerless to save themselves were the three suspected saboteurs locked in their cell. At first they must have heard the water splashing nearby, even if they couldn't see it. The single light above their heads would have soon died. No doubt they screamed for help. Their screams went unanswered.

❧

Leslie Morton, the deckhand who had first spotted the approaching torpedo, searched frantically for his brother, John. *He's off duty*, Leslie told himself, *so he could be anywhere. Where to look first? The crew quarters? Yes, that's a good idea.* He hurried forward. Already it felt as if he was running slightly downhill, but he hoped that was his imagination. He tumbled and tripped down the crazily inclined companionway. It was probably stupid to look for John. No doubt he was already safe in a lifeboat, wondering where *he* was...

He nearly knocked John down as the two met face to face on the steps. Almost in unison they told each other that the ship had been torpedoed and that they'd better get to their assigned lifeboats...

NINE-YEAR-OLD EDITH WILLIAMS STILL CLUTCHED HER sister Florence's hand. The younger girl whined; she didn't like being pulled around like a sack of potatoes. Without thinking, Edith explained that there was a problem. They had to find Mummy, but everything was going to be all right. Edith and Florence had been on deck when the torpedo hit. Within moments, chaos erupted. Where were her mother and the others? And what should they do now? Men, women and children swarmed around on the sloping deck, slipping, sliding, clutching at anything handy for support. Most of them looked dazed, as if they couldn't believe what was happening.

Edith didn't know what to do. No one helped. No one spoke to the two children. She tried to ask a sailor for advice, but he brushed past her, intent on some bigger problem. The view forward was horrifying. The ship's bow seemed to be thrusting itself into the sea. The water swirled hungrily over the wooden deck, gurgling into ventilators and hatches. Edith tugged at Florence's hand again and received a tired squeal of protest from the little girl.

"This way," Edith said. The two of them made their way up the steep incline of the deck. The gigantic funnels towered above them, symbols of strength. Instinctively Edith tried to reach them. But she pulled Florence to one side when they came alongside one of the ventilators. From the hinged lid came a horrible sound — the panicky, desperate voices of those still far below in the terrifying darkness.

Someone screamed, "She's going!"

Edith felt the deck slip away from beneath her feet.

ON SHORE THE HENDERSON FAMILY WATCHED, MESMER-ized. They had been enjoying their picnic, having traveled ten miles from Bandon on this beautiful afternoon to their favorite area near Kinsale harbor. A huge liner appeared from the west. What ship was she? *Mauretania? Britannic? Aquitania? Lusitania? Olympic?* All were British four-funnel liners, the finest vessels afloat. What a magnificent sight she was, the bright sunshine sparkling on her hull, the smoke streaming back from her tall funnels.

Then it happened. A great geyser of smoke and water burst out of the ocean and hung suspended. For a moment the ship sailed on, apparently undamaged, while the column remained stationary. An instant later a sharp crack echoed across the placid sea. The column of water collapsed.

The Hendersons couldn't believe their eyes. The inconceivable had happened right there in front of them.

In the nearby fishing village of Kinsale, the word spread quickly. The Germans had got the *Lusitania.* They'd said they would. Now they'd done it.

Someone telephoned Vice-Admiral Coke in Queenstown. An assistant took the message, but he didn't sound very convinced.

Junior Third Officer Albert Bestic waited for word to load his boat.

THE BOILER ROOMS, ALTHOUGH DAMAGED, STILL produced power. And so the ship continued to make headway. But her progress was aimless. She sailed on, turning, out of control.

Officers and crew struggled to send off the lifeboats. They found that lowering passenger-laden boats with tangled falls and a crew of ignorant, inexperienced deckhands was almost impossible. And the ship's list kept getting worse. It had turned the port side into a sloping, terrifying obstacle course of rivet heads, flanges, hatches and a thousand other projections. Most of the boats were smashed to kindling as they went slithering and sliding down the hull like toboggans gone mad, their shrieking, struggling occupants tumbling after them. In spite of the obstacles, one or two boats had, incredibly, made it down to the sea with only minor damage.

Communication on the sinking ship was confused, with orders contradicting other orders. Junior Third Officer Albert Bestic, responsible for lifeboat number ten on the port side, had been ordered not to permit passengers to board the boats. The captain hadn't given the word yet, he explained. A man swore at Bestic and yelled that lots of boats had already been launched on the starboard side. "Then go to the starboard side," Bestic shouted back. It was a bloody shambles, he thought. And a disgrace. The passengers had received no lifeboat drill. They didn't know what to do. They didn't even know how to put on their life belts. Some had them on upside down. Few of the crew were much better informed. Bestic had seen the captain only minutes before. Turner seemed unable to accept the fact that the *Lusitania* was sinking. He thought he could save her still. He didn't have a hope, in Bestic's opinion.

A man tried to climb into the boat. Bestic ordered a seaman to get him out. The seaman did as he was ordered, wielding a hefty ax within inches of the man's frightened eyes.

Farther forward a boat broke free and went skidding across the deck, slamming through the crowd of shrieking passengers.

Staff Captain Anderson appeared, disheveled and soaked. He ordered Bestic to go to the bridge and suggest to Turner that the port tanks be flooded. "It'll right the ship," he said. "Then the boats can be launched safely." He didn't sound confident.

Nurse Alice Lines took her charges on deck at the first sign of trouble.

————◄⊙►————

Bestic made his way forward, pushing through the milling throngs of frightened passengers who kept asking him what they should do, some gravely polite as if apologizing for taking up his valuable time.

"Wait for instructions," he told them. "The captain will know what's best."

Thank God no one asked *him* what was best.

Bestic scrambled up the sloping companionway, half on the steps, half on the side rails, clinging to anything at hand to maintain his balance.

At last he reached the bridge. Captain Turner stood alone, grasping the rail, staring down at the foredeck, his expression blank, as if it was all too much for him to absorb. Bestic relayed Anderson's suggestion. Turner glanced at him but didn't react. Clearly he had given up hope.

Bestic turned away. Below him the familiar deck, once so orderly, had become a madhouse. It sounded like a million birds in desperate flight. Amid a cacophony of bellowings and cries, boats went crashing into the water as passengers or sailors slashed the ropes, desperate to get away from the sinking ship. In some boats sailors searched frantically for oarlocks and oars. Others struggled to free the life rafts, using axes to smash rusty or faulty shackles. A few crewmen stood by with their arms folded, watching the nightmare unfold, as confused and uncertain as the passengers. Others saved themselves, taking rafts and abandoning the ship, ignoring passengers pleading to be saved.

❧

NURSE ALICE LINES KNEW PRECISELY WHAT HER employer, Surgeon-Major Warren Pearl, would want. She wrapped tiny Audrey in a shawl, then tied the wriggling little bundle around her neck. She took the hand of five-year-old Stuart, telling him it was time to go up on deck. Stuart grinned. He liked going up on deck.

❧

OLIVER BERNARD SAW LESLIE MASON IN THE TOPSY-turvy remains of the verandah café. Like so many others, she seemed incapable of action. When Bernard spoke to her, she just shook her head. She couldn't find her husband, she said. Tears streaked her face. Where was he? Why hadn't he stayed with her? She sounded as if she suspected Bernard of hiding him.

"Where's your life belt?" Bernard asked.

"Life belt? I don't know..."

Bernard told her to stay where she was; Stewart would be back soon. "Will he really?" she asked. No doubt about it, he assured her, promising to find her a life belt. He told her not to leave the café. She nodded.

Bernard reached the grand entrance at the head of the stairway on the boat deck and saw Alfred Vanderbilt nattily attired in a gray suit and a polka-dot tie. The multimillionaire seemed strangely amused by the confusion around him, as if it were all part of some grand show put on for his benefit. Bernard stumbled on in the gloom. He found a life belt but didn't find Leslie's husband. He hurried back to the verandah café, past masses of frightened, bewildered passengers. Where was Leslie? He was still looking for her when someone snatched the spare life belt from his hand.

❧

STUART PEARL STARTED TO CRY AS ALICE LINES TUGGED him up the stairs. He was old enough to realize that his orderly world was coming apart at the seams. Tears streamed down his cheeks, but he didn't let go of Alice's hand.

They reached the deck. Alice looked around. Where was the rest of the Pearl family? She had hoped to find the major there, hoped that he would assume responsibility for his children...

"'Ere, lad."

To Alice's alarm a sailor stooped and picked up Stuart, handing him to people in a lifeboat that was about to be launched.

Alice started to protest. Then she fell silent, deciding to follow Stuart into the boat. The children's safety was her first concern. But as she tried to climb in, an officer grabbed her arm. "You can't go in that boat, miss. It's full."

"But I must. My boy is in there."

He shook his head, his mouth set in an obstinate line. He turned to the seamen.

"Lower away!"

Alice glimpsed the boat swaying out over the churning water. There was no time to think. No time for anything but doing what had to be done.

She leaped off the deck, reaching desperately for the boat now suspended in space. A sailor glanced at her, his mouth dropping open. Behind him a woman stared at her in disbelief.

At that moment Alice knew she had miscalculated. The boat swung away from her as she jumped. Her fingers brushed its smooth painted surface. She couldn't grab it. She glimpsed the water — the splashing, frantic people, the incredible assortment of floating junk. Directly below her she saw an enormous packing case. She winced, thinking she was going to hit it. She missed. Just. But when she struck the water, the impact knocked the breath out of her. Gasping, spluttering, she went under, fighting to remain conscious. She still clutched baby Audrey in a bundle around her neck.

Alice opened her eyes under water. She saw her own hair streaming about her, waving like a banner. Normally she wore it in a bun, but there hadn't been time to put it up before she had rushed up to the deck.

It may have saved her life and Audrey's.

As she broke the surface, strong fingers grabbed her flowing hair. It hurt like the devil. She opened her mouth to protest, but water poured in, choking her.

She saw sunlight and faces. A hand caught her shoulder.

"C'mon, ducks."

Then Alice was in the boat, sprawled across people, coughing the seawater out of her.

In the rush, many boats were dropped into the water, spilling their human cargo. Others were lowered on those already in the water.

T oward the end, the Lusitania *began slipping away on a shallow angle. Many lifeboats remained unlaunched and hundreds of people were washed off the decks in the final moments.*

littered the water. There were such desperate struggles as I shall never forget. Many were entangled between chairs, rafts, and upturned boats. One by one they seemed to fall off and give themselves up to death. One poor wretch was struck by the oar which I was sharing with a steward. We struck him full in the head but he

O nce she had gone, eyewitnesses reported that an enormous

seized and clung to the oar like grim death until we were able to drag him into the boat. Next we saw a woman floating quite near us. Her face was just visible above the water, and her mouth was covered with froth." Bernard and the others pulled the woman aboard, but she died within minutes.

mass of foaming water appeared in the sea, probably the last air escaping from the liner. (Right) Everywhere, those in the water saw the trail of the great ship marked out in wreckage and bodies.

EIGHTEEN MINUTES AFTER SCHWIEGER'S TORPEDO struck her, the Lusitania began her final journey. Her stern rose out of the water, the propellers turning wearily.

A score of tiny figures, arms fluttering, leaped from her upper decks. They were the last to leave, and most of them went down with her.

Third Officer Albert Bestic saw the ship sink. He watched, fascinated yet horrified. For a few heart-stopping moments she was stationary, poised, preparing for her final plunge. Bestic wondered if her bow had already hit the bottom of the sea, only some fifty fathoms deep at that point.

A series of great thuds and bangs shook the Lusitania's elegant hull. Bestic grimaced, picturing the chaos aboard her, imagining how massive pieces of heavy machinery must be tearing away and plunging

forward, eviscerating everything in their path.

Then, at last, she settled.

A moment after the stern vanished beneath the surface, a great round mountain of water erupted "with huge globules of white foam." It seemed to hang there motionless, a man's body bobbing spread-eagled in the midst of it.

It was all over. The hill of water subsided with a dull roar, sending echoes of itself in every direction. Bestic felt himself being lifted by the swell. Around him bodies — some living, some apparently dead — bobbed like dolls in life belts.

Bestic wore no life belt. He had intended to get one before diving into the sea, but he never had the chance. The ship simply sank away beneath him. One moment he was on the deck, the next the water reached up to grab him and he found himself swimming for his life, wishing he had thought to kick off his shoes while he had the chance. The damned things felt like lead weights on his feet. He had vaguely expected to be sucked down when the ship sank. He'd been lucky to escape.

Bestic looked around him. There were hundreds of heads in every direction. Hands reached up, grasping at nothing. Voices, weak and without hope, called for help. Instinctively he started to swim in the direction of the Irish coastline, at least ten miles away. Deadly, numbing fatigue quickly overcame him. He lost track of why he was here and where he was going. Did he have a life outside all this? Maybe so, but the details eluded him. The distinction between reality and fantasy was blurring.

He collided with something. Weakly he reached out and found his fingers grasping a gunwale. A boat! Pretty badly bashed in, but still afloat.

It took the last of his strength to drag himself

halfway out of the water. Heaven knows how long he lay there, his legs trailing in the sea, reveling in the sheer delight of not having to swim, just letting his leaden limbs flop as if the bones had turned to rubber. He slept, dreaming of home and the dry, warm hearth and drinking a piping-hot cup of cocoa before going to bed. He may have slept for half an hour or perhaps only a few seconds; he didn't know. In any event he awoke abruptly when salty water began licking around his mouth and nose. He opened his eyes. For a crazy instant he didn't know where he was. Then he remembered and the memories hit him one after the other like sharp blows. Simultaneously he realized something important: the bloody boat was sinking! A steady stream of water was pouring in through a jagged hole in the bow.

Bestic set to work to patch the boat with bits and pieces of wood and cork and other debris that floated by. He helped a dark-haired young man aboard the fragile vessel. Shivering, teeth chattering, the young man thanked Bestic with some formality and asked if he had any cigarettes.

Bestic reached into his pocket and produced a pulpy mess of paper and bits of tobacco.

The two of them spluttered with laughter; the remains of Bestic's cigarettes suddenly seemed to be the funniest sight either of them had ever seen. They were still chuckling when they came across a woman in the water, feebly trying to swim, supported in an awkward, lopsided way by a life jacket that had almost slipped from her shoulders. She kept mumbling something, her voice husky with exhaustion. They dragged her aboard. She demanded to know where her baby was. The two men said they hadn't seen any babies.

With a despairing moan the woman pulled herself to the side of the boat and dropped back into the water. The men grabbed her and pulled her aboard again.

"I'm wrong," said the young dark-haired man. He told her the child was safe. "It's in another boat. Just over there. Not far."

He was lying, but it seemed like the right thing to say.

❧

EDITH WILLIAMS FELT HERSELF BEING SWEPT ALONG LIKE a soap bubble in the bath water rushing toward a gulping, gurgling drain. She was helpless and alone. Florence's hand had slipped from hers in the fierce assault of water — a great, overwhelming tide that was too powerful to resist.

THE LADY VANISHES

❶ *The* Lusitania's *death throes begin after the second explosion set off by the torpedo.*

❷ *Still plowing ahead, the ship starts to list.*

❸ *Then, righting slightly, she sails under the waves, toward the bottom.*

❹ *The last air bursts from the ship, and she hits the seafloor on her starboard side.*

Although the Lusitania *sank* on a warm spring day, the water off southern Ireland is cold at that time of year. For many of the people (below and bottom) struggling in the water, death from exposure was to be their fate.

Edith struggled, sucking in more water than air. *I'm drowning*, she thought. *In a moment I will be dead.* Oddly, the thought seemed to belong to someone else.

At that instant she glimpsed a woman clinging to a rope that was attached to some floating wreckage. Edith reached out. Her fingers grasped rough, tweedy material. It was the woman's skirt, and it saved her.

THE *LUSITANIA* WAS GONE. HER DEATH AGONY WAS over. The water bubbled and gurgled, recovering from the shock of it all. Smoke and steam hung over the spot as if marking it for eternity. In a few minutes the waters were still, leaving the living and dead, the debris, the clouds of soot from the engine room, the sad reminders that a great and proud ship had died here.

QUEENSTOWN WAS IN SHOCK. THE unthinkable had happened. The *Lusitania* had gone down on the small town's doorstep, so to speak. How many hundreds had gone with her?

By late afternoon the first of the small armada of tugs and trawlers were returning, some with corpses aboard, some with survivors, some with both. In many cases it was hard to tell them apart.

Margaret Mackworth awoke to find herself lying naked between two rough blankets. She must have lost consciousness in the water; she had vague, dreamlike memories of floating, feeling as if she was freezing to death, being dragged around like a prize salmon. What had happened? And when? It felt like ten years. Time seemed to have become twisted out of shape.

A sailor appeared, a cheerful-looking man with bright blue eyes. "That's better," he said.

She was going to ask what was better, but it didn't seem worth the trouble.

It was then that she realized that she was outside. It wasn't a hard bunk she was lying on, but a deck. The blackness above was the night sky, not the ceiling of a room.

"Like a cup of tea, ducks?"

"Where am I?" Her teeth began to chatter uncontrollably; they sounded like a military drummer clattering away for all his might in her head. Pain stabbed the small of her back.

"You're on the *Bluebell*. We picked you up."

"I don't remember."

"Not surprised," said the sailor conversationally. "Matter of fact we thought you was dead. That's why we left you on deck. Didn't seem worthwhile cumbering up the cabin with you," he added with a friendly grin.

Helped by three sailors, Margaret made her way below to the bright warmth of the captain's cabin. They put her into a warm, cozy bunk. She had no idea how long she slept. And when she finally came to, it wasn't the babble of voices that woke her, it was the smell of pipe tobacco — a coarse, pungent smell that tickled her nose. She opened her eyes. People crammed the tiny cabin, all survivors by the look of them and the chaotic assortment of garments they wore. Everyone was

Alerted by the Lusitania's *distress calls and eyewitnesses ashore, many vessels showed up. In reality, the majority were fishing vessels, not the naval ships shown here.*

talking at once, frequently spluttering into high-pitched, hysterical laughter. A woman told Margaret that her husband was almost certainly dead. He was, she said, all she had in the world. Her voice was emotionless; it was as if the enormity of the event had stunned her.

Another voice cut through the chatter, the voice of a man so emotional that his words came in angry spurts. The whole sorry episode was a disgrace, he snapped. A crime! The world would soon know who was responsible. No discipline! No organization!

It took a moment for Margaret to realize at whom the comments were directed. Then she saw him sitting in a corner of the cabin, a blanket around his hunched shoulders, his eyes downcast. It was Turner. Captain Turner.

THE QUEENSTOWN HARBOR official wouldn't let anyone land. No, he declared, shaking his head in the righteously obstinate way of minor bureaucrats the world over. The necessary papers had not been completed and filed, and there was no one present who could authorize an unscheduled landing.

But his resistance began to crumble as the boats kept coming in and the crews kept depositing their pathetic catch on the harbor steps. The victims lay in untidy rows with staring eyes and frozen grimaces. There were scores of them, men, women and the tiniest of children; saloon, second-cabin and third-class passengers; stewards and stokers, officers and musicians. So rigidly segregated a few hours earlier, they now lay together, victims all.

Leslie Morton made his careful way along the untidy rows of sodden bodies on the harbor steps. There hadn't been time to do more than toss a blanket over the naked corpses or those with particularly hideous injuries. The others lay as they had emerged from the sea, dirt and soot still caked on their features. Leslie gazed at each waxen face in turn. He soon discovered a grotesque truth: recognizing a dead person was no easy task. Death had stamped the faces with a certain ghastly sameness, male and female, young and old. Could that one be his brother John? It appalled him that he could be uncertain. He knew John as well as he knew himself. Yet the fact remained that he was frequently unsure. That one *could* be John. So could that one. He chided himself for talking about the corpses as things. Who knew what horrors some of these poor devils had gone through, if their expressions and their twisted limbs were anything to go by. He prayed that John had died quickly, painlessly.

Townsfolk drifted down to the harbor, aghast yet fascinated. They talked quietly among themselves, as if afraid of disturbing the corpses. The know-it-alls who invariably appeared at such moments said they had been expecting this all along. They had been spotting submarines in the waters off Queenstown for a week or more. The subs had been waiting for the *Lusitania*, they declared.

More boats came in. More bodies were deposited

THE MAN WHO COULD NOT BE DROWNED?

H e was the luckiest man on the *Lusitania*. A middle-aged fireman in the engine room, a plain-spoken person with dirt under his fingernails, not the sort to attract a second glance on that luxury liner. But he deserved one, for he possessed the devil's own luck. His name was Frank Tower. Once a member of the crew of the *Titanic*, he had made his escape from that doomed ship as she sank in the Atlantic after hitting an iceberg. Two years later, he was working aboard the Canadian Pacific liner *Empress of Ireland* when she collided in thick fog with the Norwegian collier *Storstad*. The liner sank in the St. Lawrence with the loss of over a thousand lives, but Tower survived. Then in May 1915, he was a member of the *Lusitania*'s engine room crew when the *U-20* torpedoed her. Again, he came through without a scratch.

If it all seemed a little too good to be true, it was. Research reveals no Frank Tower listed among the crew of the *Lusitania*. Or the *Empress of Ireland*. Or the *Titanic*. And even his name seems open to question. The man at left, who is identified as the survivor of those three wrecks, is called Turner. And no stoker called Turner ever served on those three ships, either. In the end the tale seems to be an urban folk myth, arising, perhaps, out of our desire to see people triumph in the face of terrible tragedies.

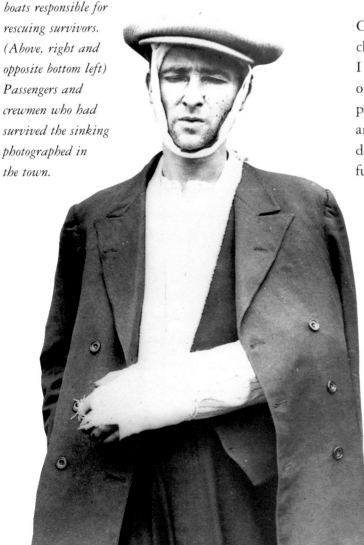

S mall boys play in the Lusitania *lifeboats (left) that had been towed into Queenstown. (Opposite bottom right) Some of the local fishing boats responsible for rescuing survivors. (Above, right and opposite bottom left) Passengers and crewmen who had survived the sinking photographed in the town.*

with sad, wet plops on the stone. Policemen and soldiers stood guard, their faces expressionless.

IT WAS DARK WHEN THE *BLUEBELL* PULLED INTO Queenstown. Margaret Mackworth tried to get out of the bunk, but her limbs wouldn't cooperate. She found that she was bruised from head to foot. And filthy. The skipper said he would get someone to help her out of the bunk. Margaret pointed out that she had no clothes. The skipper nodded and said he would see what he could find.

A moment later a familiar face appeared. It was the steward from the *Lusitania*'s first-class dining room, a tall, thin man with a melancholy voice. Now a ghost of a smile haunted a corner of his mouth.

"I thought you'd like to know, madam. Your father's been rescued. He's safe and sound," he said.

OLIVER BERNARD COULDN'T TEAR THE IMAGES OF THE children's corpses from his mind. "A number of babies, I should say about thirty, were laid out stark and stiff on the floor of a temporary morgue," he told a newspaper reporter. "I never saw anything quite so ghastly and harrowing, and it filled me with an insensate desire for vengeance. I hope those tiny mites will be fully avenged."

Early the next day cartloads of coffins arrived at Queenstown while British troops were put to work digging graves in the churchyard. The town hall became a huge morgue. Counting and identifying the dead became the chief business of the town's bureaucracy. Coffins replaced desks. A steady line of survivors and relatives proceeded hesitantly through the offices and meeting rooms now reeking of seawater and death.

Some of the victims wore peaceful expressions. One or two looked astonished, as if they had died not quite believing what had happened to them. Others seemed to have died mouthing oaths, fighting to the last. Several mothers and children lay in one another's arms.

LESLIE MORTON STILL HADN'T FOUND HIS BROTHER. He had been up all night and now, in the light of the new day, he was still at it, inspecting each new batch of bodies as they came in. "They're picking 'em up from as far away as Hook Head," a soldier on guard remarked conversationally.

Leslie ignored him. He kept looking, lifting up the corners of sheets, gazing at the frozen, colorless features beneath. He had to force himself to pay attention to each one, resisting the temptation to glance quickly at each body and say no. He was lifting the corner of one sheet when he sensed someone lifting the other side. It was John, grinning broadly, looking comical in an ill-fitting checkered suit. Both wanted to know where the devil the other had been; they had been searching for each other for hours.

"Where did you get that horrible suit?"

"Somebody gave it to me. Someone from Cunard, I think."

"If I were you," said Leslie, "I'd give it back."

❧

HOUR AFTER HOUR SOLEMN CLUSTERS OF people continued to move among the coffins, timorously lifting corners of sheets and looking apprehensively at the victims beneath. A number of children were involved in this ghastly duty. Some sobbed, shaking their heads, protesting as they were led from coffin to coffin.

For a moment Chrissie Aitken didn't recognize her father. This pallid, taut-featured person with the mocking grin fixed on his thin lips seemed to have no connection with the warm-hearted man who had once been the focus of her existence.

"That's him. My father. James Aitken."

"You're sure?"

Among the 123 Americans who died were author Elbert Hubbard (top) and playwright Charles Klein (above).

"Yes, sir."

"Well done," muttered the official, as if she had passed a difficult test at school. He moved off, writing something on his clipboard. She watched him go. Her father was dead, her brother and his son were missing. What, she wondered, was she supposed to do next?

❧

ALFRED VANDERBILT AND CHARLES FROHMAN, THE two most famous passengers on board the *Lusitania*, both lost their lives. According to eyewitnesses, neither seemed to make any effort to save himself. Vanderbilt, who despite his other athletic accomplishments couldn't swim a stroke, was last seen instructing his valet to find life belts for children who needed them. Frohman apparently went down with the ship, quoting lines from *Peter Pan*, one of his greatest theatrical successes. His body was later found; Vanderbilt's never was. Other American victims included the Cromptons of Philadelphia and their six children; Elbert Hubbard, the noted author and publisher; newlyweds Stewart and Leslie Mason; and Charles Klein, co-author of the play *Potash and Perlmutter*, then playing at London's Queen's Theatre and one of the hits of the season.

❧

ON THE EVENING OF MAY 8, MARGARET Mackworth and her father, David Thomas, were reunited with Howard Fisher and Dorothy Conner. The four of them sat down to dinner once again — not in the domed splendor of the *Lusitania*'s dining room, but in a seedy little Queenstown hotel. Although the meal was mediocre, the occasion was memorable. They talked for hours about their experiences and agreed that they were among the luckiest of the passengers aboard the ill-fated liner. They chuckled over

The flag-draped body of an American casualty is carried through the streets of Queenstown.

the headline in a Welsh newspaper: GREAT NATIONAL DISASTER. D.A. THOMAS SAVED. Then they said good-bye. The Americans went on to France; Margaret and her father went home to Wales.

❧

NO SOONER HAD OLIVER BERNARD ARRIVED IN LONDON than *The Illustrated London News* contacted him and asked him to sketch his impressions of the sinking. He obliged, thinking the drawings would be used simply as a guide for a professional illustrator. He was surprised to see them reproduced as is in the May 15 issue.

❧

TWO DAYS AFTER SHE STEPPED ASHORE AT QUEENSTOWN, Chrissie Aitken walked up a quiet residential street in Edinburgh. She still wore the clothes she had been wearing when the *Lusitania* went down. The stylish

hobble skirt she had been so proud of was wrinkled and shapeless now. All her other clothes had gone down with the ship. No one had offered her any assistance. She had walked around Queenstown for a few hours, eventually arriving at the railway station. She had enough money to buy a ticket to Edinburgh. Now, at last, she was at her aunt and uncle's home.

She rapped on the door. The instant her aunt opened it, her face paled and her eyes opened wide. For a moment she couldn't say anything. Then, over a hot cup of tea, the story came out. A man from a newspaper had been at the house only a few hours before. He had told her aunt and uncle that all the Aitkens had been lost on the *Lusitania*. Her aunt could scarcely believe her ears. Until the reporter's arrival, she hadn't even known that any of her family were on the ship.

Chapter Six

Pointing *the* Finger

I T WAS THE BIGGEST STORY OF THE YEAR. IN London the newspapers exploded with righteous indignation, talking of the "moral degradation" of a nation that could perpetrate such a crime: "a dastardly, piratical act," "the foulest of the many foul crimes that have stained German arms," "the ghastliest crime in history."

Mobs stormed through the streets of London, Manchester, Liverpool and other major British cities, hurling bricks through the windows of shops and restaurants with German names, stealing merchandise in some cases, setting fires in others. Hotels refused rooms to people named Muller or Schultz, even if they could produce documents proving British citizenship. Homes were wrecked, vehicles vandalized; and, according to more than one report, a few mentally deficient patriots did their bit for the cause by chasing dachshunds in the street and kicking them.

Most Americans felt similar repulsion. Fiery ex-president Theodore Roosevelt called the sinking "piracy on a vaster scale than any old-time pirate ever practiced," adding that it was inconceivable "that we can refrain from

In London, crowds gathered outside the Cunard office for news of the sinking. (Opposite) Enraged by the disaster, angry British mobs attacked businesses with German names, in this case ransacking a German-owned barbershop.

"All the News That's Fit to Print."

The New York Times.

EXTRA
5:30 A.M.

Weather Today and Sunday Fair.

VOL. LXIV...NO. 20,923. •••••   NEW YORK, SATURDAY, MAY 8, 1915.—TWENTY-FOUR PAGES.   ONE CENT In Greater New York, Jersey City and Newark.   Elsewhere TWO CENTS.

LUSITANIA SUNK BY A SUBMARINE, PROBABLY 1,260 DEAD;
TWICE TORPEDOED OFF IRISH COAST; SINKS IN 15 MINUTES;
CAPT. TURNER SAVED, FROHMAN AND VANDERBILT MISSING;
WASHINGTON BELIEVES THAT A GRAVE CRISIS IS AT HAND

SHOCKS THE PRESIDENT

Washington Deeply Stirred by the Loss of American Lives.

BULLETINS AT WHITE HOUSE

Wilson Reads Them Closely, but Is Silent on the Nation's Course.

HINTS OF CONGRESS CALL

Loss of Lusitania Recalls Firm Tone of Our First Warning to Germany.

CAPITAL FULL OF RUMORS

Reports That Liner Was to be Sunk Were Heard Before Actual News Came.

Special to The New York Times.

WASHINGTON, May 7.—Never since that April day, three years ago, when word came that the Titanic had gone down, has Washington been so stirred as it is tonight over the sinking of the Lusitania. The early reports told that there had been no loss of life, but the relief that these advices caused gave way to the greatest concern late this evening when it became known that there had been many deaths. Although they are profoundly reticent, officials realize that this tragedy, involving the loss of American citizens, is likely to bring about a crisis in the international relations of the United States.

It is pointed out that the sinking of the Lusitania is the outcome of a series of incidents that have been the cause of concern to this Government in its endeavor to maintain a strictly neutral position in the great European war.

Nation's Course in Doubt.

It is impossible to say tonight what effect the loss of American lives on the Lusitania will have on the Government. Judged from the little that can be learned it is a safe prediction that President Wilson will endeavor to ascertain all the facts, including evidence as to whether a German submarine was responsible for the sinking of the vessel, before proceeding to determine the course to be pursued. The news that many lives had been sacrificed, probably as many as a thousand, was given to him at the White House about 10 o'clock this morning, but no word came from him as to what effect this intelligence had on him.

The State Department tonight sent instructions to the American Embassy in London to send the names of any Americans who might have been killed or injured in the disaster. A bulletin from The Times, saying probably 1,000 lives had been lost, was sent to the White House as soon as received and laid before President Wilson. The news that two torpedoes had been fired into the Lusitania by a submarine and that the Lusitania sank fifteen minutes afterward was also sent to the White House, but reached there after the President had gone to bed. The President retired about 11 o'clock.

On account of the many inquiries it had received from friends and relatives of passengers on the Lusitania and the intense public interest in the tragedy, orders were given tonight to the telegraphers and cipher clerks in charge of the telegraph office in the State Department to remain at their posts all night. They also had instructions to make public any messages bringing official details regarding the Lusitania's passengers. Usually the telegraph office closes at midnight.

Rumors of Congress Session.

There were reports this evening that Congress would be called in extra session, but these were not justified while the Government is greatly concerned over the situation, it has shown no inclination toward excitement or taking hasty action. Senator by J. Stone, Chairman of the Committee on Foreign Relations, said tonight:

"I cannot comment on a supposed

Continued on Page 4.

Cunard Office Here Besieged for News; Fate of 1,918 on Lusitania Long in Doubt

Nothing Heard from the Well-Known Passengers on Board—Story of Disaster Long Unconfirmed While Anxious Crowds Seek Details.

Official news of the sinking of the Lusitania yesterday reached New York in fragmentary reports, and several hours elapsed between the first unverified rumor of the disaster and the cable messages that told at night of the saving of some of the passengers and gave meagre details of the most sensational incident of its kind in the war.

The early accounts that indicated all on board had been saved because hundreds of friends and relatives of passengers. Later it was made known that lives had been lost and probably many persons had been injured.

Among the prominent passengers rescued was George A Kessler. The list of those of whom no word was received included A G Vanderbilt, Charles Frohman, Charles Klein, Justus Miles Forman, and Elbert Hubbard, besides persons widely known in society.

A cablegram sent to Farley Hopkins of The Yale News staff at New Haven by his father who was aboard the Lusitania, stated that the vessel was sunk not beached. that three hundred persons had been already landed, and the intention of keeping back the news from the public. Several bulletins were received from the Liverpool office, but few of them contained any definite statements and they were cancelled, in some instances, within an hour. One received at 4:37 M read

Message to Cunard Office.

The first word of the sinking of the Lusitania received here reached the local offices of the Cunard Line, 21 State Street, at 11:43 o'clock yesterday morning, but was not made public until late in the afternoon. The message, which was sent from the head office in Liverpool, read:

> Liverpool, May 7.
> 131 P M (New York Time.)
> Queenstown station reports Lusitania sunk. Several boats apparently coming southeast here. Fishing boats are making for the spot to render assistance.

The next bulletin made public at the Cunard office was the following:

> Liverpool, May 7.
> 131 P M (New York Times.)
> Lusitania in no news as to the safety of passengers or crew

The next bulletin read:

Continued on Page 3.

List of Saved Includes Capt. Turner; Vanderbilt and Frohman Reported Lost

LONDON, Saturday, May 8, 5:30 A. M.—The Press Bureau has received from the British Admiralty at Queenstown a report that all the torpedo boats and tugs and armed trawlers, except the Heron, which went out from Queenstown to the relief of the Lusitania have returned.

These vessels have landed 595 survivors and forty dead. Fifty-two more survivors are reported aboard a steamer, while eleven others and five bodies have been landed at Kinsale, making the total number of survivors 658, besides forty-five dead. The numbers will be verified later, and it is considered possible Kinsale fishing boats may have rescued a few more.

Among the survivors is the Captain of the Lusitania, William T Turner. Some of the survivors at Queenstown say that Alfred Gwynne Vanderbilt was drowned. Every effort to find Mr. Vanderbilt and Charles Frohman, the theatrical manager, among the survivors has failed.

QUEENSTOWN, Saturday, May 8, 4:45 A. M.—The list of the Lusitania's survivors, as far as compiled, follows:

TURNER, Captain.
ABRAMOWITZ, A. T. Montreal.
ABRAHAMOVITZ, S.
LANE, O. B.
MEYERS, W. G. E.
TRIMEINE, J. T.
WITHERBEE, Mrs. A. F
MACKWORTH, Lady.
ADAMS, Mrs. HENRY, Boston
RANKIN, ROBERT, New York.
SHARP, SAMUEL.
BYRNE, M. H. New York
DAVIS, EMILY.
MANGER, ANNIE.
HOUSSELL, K.
CROSS, A. B.
YOUNG, PHILIP, Montreal
VASSAR, W. A. F. London
STEELE, GEORGE.
CROSLEY, CYRUS.
PARKER, JAMES.
COLEBROOK, the Rev. R. I.
MORRIS, H. C. S.
FISH, Mrs. and two children.
MARTIN, Miss B.
GATTLETT, P. J. New York
MAYDOCK, Miss MAY
HENDERSON, UNO.
MARBERIO, UNO.
LEVIN, THOMAS D.
THOMAS, D. A. Cardiff, Wales
EVANS, T. J. M.
CLARKE, A. N.
BURGESS, W. O.
CHARLES, B. H. and daughter.
Toronto
LOVRY, Miss. New York
HERBIE, JOHN.
HOLLAND, Miss.
BRANDELL, Miss JOSEPHINE.
New York
PERRY, F. K A
GRAB, O. H.
MOSLEY, G. O., New York.
BROOKS, J. H., New York
JEFFEY, A. M
CAIRNS, M
HAMMOND, O. H. New York
MANLEY, A.
NEATH, H
NORTH, Miss.
WINTER, Miss.
WINTER, Mrs.
DUGUID, GEORGE
MOORE, DANIEL.
MCCONNELL, JOHN W., Memphis, Tenn.
SHARPE, Miss.
CONNER, Miss.
DAILY, H. H.
CLIFFE, PATRICK
BOHAN, JAMES, Toronto
CROSLEY, Mrs. CYRUS
BRETHERTON, Mrs. CYRIL H
and two children Los Angeles
Cal.
HOPKINS, A L. New York
LASSETTER, Mrs. H R. of Sydney, Australia, wife of General Lassetter
LASSETTER Master P

LAURIAT, CHARLES E., Jr., Boston, Mass
PAYNTER, Miss IRENE, Liverpool, England.

KINSALE, Ireland, May 8.—Eleven survivors of the Lusitania have been landed here, together with the bodies of five persons who were dead. Among the survivors are:
SMITH, J. RESTON New York
BOTTOMLEY, FREDERICK
BOYLE, N. J.
HUTCHINGS, CHARLES.
HARRISON, CORNELIUS.
LIVERMORE, VERNAL
SULLIVAN, Mrs. F.

Consul's List of Saved.

WASHINGTON, May 8.—Consul Lauriat at Queenstown sends this report:

"Total saved of all nationalities, 700. The following are American survivors of Lusitania. Other names will follow:
CRAB, O. B
PEARL, Major and Mrs. and two children
SMITH, Mrs. JESSIE TAFT
HARDWICK, CHARLES C
EARL, STUART D
PEARL, AMY
STANLEY, Mrs.
LINES, L. B
HILL, C. T.
RANKIN, ROBERT
LANEY, Miss.
DOHERTY, Mrs. WILLIAM and infant.
PHILLIPS, THOMAS
McADAMS, WILLIAM
HOUGHTON, J. R
SWEENEY, JOHN M.
HAMMOND, OADEN H
BROOKS, J. H
JEFFEY CHARLES T
LYND, Mrs. C. H
SHEPPERDSON, ARTHUR
MOORE, Dr D V
DONALD, CLINTON.
LIGHT, HERBERT
LENNOX, J. D.
WILLIAMS, JOHN
HOLLAND, Mrs. JOHN
MIESH, Mrs. NINA
KESSLER, GEORGE A
McMURRAY, L
MAY, ROBERT
LOCKHART, H. J.
CANNON, OWEN
HARRIS, DWIGHT G
HUDSON, FRED S
COLLIS, ED H.
KNOX, R. G
WRIGHT, R. C
GAUNTLET, F. J.
O'CONNELL, PATRICK.

Saw the Submarine 100 Yards Off and Watched Torpedo as It Struck Ship

Ernest Cowper, a Toronto Newspaper Man, Describes Attack, Seen from Ship's Rail—Poison Gas Used in Torpedoes, Say Other Passengers.

Queenstown, Saturday, May 8, 3:18 A. M.

A sharp lookout for submarines was kept aboard the Lusitania as she approached the Irish coast, according to Ernest Cowper, a Toronto newspaper man, who was among the survivors landed at Queenstown.

He said that after the ship was torpedoed there was no panic among the crew, but that they went about the work of getting passengers into the boats in a prompt and efficient manner.

"As we neared the coast of Ireland," said Mr Cowper, "we all joined in the lookout, for a possible attack by a submarine was the sole topic of conversation.

"I was chatting with a friend at the rail about 2 o'clock when suddenly I caught a glimpse of the submarine about a thousand yards distant. I immediately called my friend's attention to it. Immediately we both saw the track of a torpedo followed almost instantly by an explosion. Portions of splintered hull were sent flying into the air, and then another torpedo struck. The ship began to list to starboard.

"The crew at once proceeded to get the passengers into boats in an orderly, prompt, and efficient manner Miss Helen Smith appealed to me to save her. I placed her in a boat and saw her safely away I got into one of the last boats to leave.

"Some of the boats could not be launched as the vessel was sinking. There was a large number of women and children in the second cabin. Forty of the children were less than a year old."

Poison Fumes from Torpedoes.

From interviews with passengers it appears that when the torpedoes burst they sent forth suffocating fumes which had their effect on the passengers, causing some of them to lose consciousness.

Two stokers, Byrne and Hussey of Liverpool, gave a few details. They said the submarine gave no notice and fired two torpedoes, one hitting No. 1 stoke hole and the second the engine room. The first torpedo was discharged at 2 o'clock. In twenty-five minutes the great liner disappeared.

Signals have been received at Queenstown that an armed trawler, believed to be the Heron, and two fishing trawlers are bringing in 100 more bodies.

The Cunard Line agent states that the total number of persons aboard the Lusitania was 2,160

Loss of the Lusitania Fills London With Horror and Utter Amazement

Special Cable to The New York Times.

LONDON Saturday May 8.—Stupefaction is the word which best describes the first impression created by the news of the sinking of the Lusitania. People seemed unable to realise that at this stage of the world's progress such a deed could be committed as an act of war.

"I have no words for it," said Lord Beresbury and everywhere one found the same sentiment repeated.

It was some hours between the time

Continued on Page 2.

The Lost Cunard Steamship Lusitania
X Where the First Torpedo Struck.   XX Where the Second Torpedo Struck.

SOME DEAD TAKEN ASHORE

Several Hundred Survivors at Queenstown and Kinsale.

STEWARD TELLS OF DISASTER

One Torpedo Crashes Into the Doomed Liner's Bow, Another Into the Engine Room.

SHIP LISTS OVER TO PORT

Makes It Impossible to Lower Many Boats, So Hundreds Must Have Gone Down.

ATTACKED IN BROAD DAY

Passengers at Luncheon—Warning Had Been Given by Germans Before the Ship Left New York.

Only 650 Were Saved, Few Cabin Passengers

QUEENSTOWN, Saturday, May 8, 4:28 A. M.—Survivors of the Lusitania who have arrived here estimate that only about 650 of those aboard the steamer were saved, and say only a small proportion of those rescued were saloon passengers.

Official Confirmation

WASHINGTON, May 8.—A dispatch to the State Department early today from American Consul Lauriet at Queenstown stated that the total number of survivors of the Lusitania was about 700.

LONDON, Saturday, May 8.—The Cunard liner Lusitania which sailed out of New York last Saturday with 1,918 souls aboard, lies at the bottom of the ocean off the Irish coast.

She was sunk by a German submarine, which sent two torpedoes crashing into her side at 2:30 o'clock yesterday afternoon while the passengers seemingly confident that the great swift vessel could elude the German underwater craft were having luncheon.

The great inrush of water caused the liner to list heavily to port, so that she could not launch many of her lifeboats.

About 1,260 of those on board the great ship, including many Americans, apparently went down with her, as a statement issued late this morning by the Admiralty says the total number of survivors is only 658.

There were 1,253 passengers on board the steamship, including 200 who were transferred to her from the steamer Cameronia. The Americans totaled 188. The crew numbered 665.

It is believed that only a few first class passengers were saved as they thought the ship would remain afloat, and made little effort to escape.

There appears to be a large proportion of the survivors among those landed at Queenstown. Only a few off

LUSITANIA TORPEDOED BY GERMAN PIRATE

The Daily Mirror

CERTIFIED CIRCULATION LARGER THAN ANY OTHER PICTURE PAPER IN THE WORLD

No. 3,000.   SATURDAY, MAY 8, 1915   **16 PAGES**   One Halfpenny.

THE HUNS CARRY OUT THEIR THREAT TO MURDER : FAMOUS CUNARDER SUNK OFF THE IRISH COAST.

HOW THE LUSITANIA WAS SUNK.

DAILY SKETCH.

GUARANTEED DAILY NETT SALE MORE THAN **1,000,000** COPIES.

No. 1,923.   LONDON, SATURDAY, MAY 8, 1915.   One Halfpenny.

THE HUNS SINK THE LUSITANIA.

Illustrierte Unterhaltungs=Beilage

Der Tag

Zum Untergang der „Lusitania": Rettungsboote verlassen das sinkende Schiff.

News of the sinking took over the front pages of newspapers in most of the English-speaking world. Reactions ranged from the New York Times' warning of an impending grave crisis to the British tabloids' denunciations of murder by the Huns. German papers (left) also covered the story, although from a different angle.

taking action on this matter, for we owe it not only to humanity but to our national self-respect." The American ambassador in London cabled Washington: "The U.S. must declare war or forfeit European respect." There was a feeling of personal involvement in the tragedy, since so many of the victims were compatriots. The New York papers talked of the Germans making war "like savages drunk with blood." The *Times* declared ringingly, "In the history of wars there is no single deed comparable in its inhumanity and its horror." "Premeditated slaughter," the *New York Herald* called it.

L usitania *survivors line up for tickets at the Queenstown train station (left). (Above) A group of passengers on their arrival at London's Waterloo Station. The man on the right still clutches his life jacket.*

The *Louisville Courier-Journal* dubbed Germany "the nation of the Black Hand and Bloody Heart." The Baltimore *Sun* talked of the sinking marking a "return to the most brutal practices of barbarism."

What appalled just about everybody was that the splendid liner, packed with civilians, many of them neutrals, had been torpedoed without warning. Civilized people simply couldn't do such things. Inevitably editorialists roped in analogies from the sports world, where the rules of conduct were clearly understood by all participants. The Ottawa *Citizen* described the sinking as a "blow beneath the belt." However, the editorial assured readers that the despicable act would do the Hun no good: "The hard-headed Britisher does not give up when struck a foul blow."

The fact that the Germans had placed advertisements in the papers warning travelers of the dangers of sailing on British ships only seemed to make the whole thing that much more reprehensible. It smacked of the taunting notes that Jack the Ripper had sent to Scotland Yard. President Woodrow Wilson himself made the point with admirable clarity when he declared that "no warning that that unlawful and inhumane act will be committed" excused the act itself.

In those early, relatively innocent years of the twentieth century, Americans as a whole were convinced that, war or no war, they had an inalienable right to travel with perfect safety on any nation's ships. Similarly they believed that U.S. vessels should be able to journey unharmed through war zones. The war was Europe's business, not America's. Three months before, in February 1915, the Germans had declared the seas all around the British Isles a war zone. Enemy vessels, armed or unarmed, would be destroyed, warned Berlin. Neutral shipping was also at risk, it was explained, because of the misuse of neutral flags by the British. Wilson informed the Germans that they would be held to "strict accountability" if their actions resulted in American ships or lives being lost. No doubt the majority of his compatriots thought Wilson a hell of a fellow. Like a sheriff of the Old West he had laid down the law; he had drawn his line in the dust. *Step over this, Fritz, and you've got trouble.* But what did "strict accountability" mean? Wilson had talked of taking any steps "it might be necessary to take" to safeguard American lives and property. Was this a warning that he would declare war on Germany if Americans lost their lives because of German action? And how far did Wilson think his warning went?

On May 1, the day of the *Lusitania*'s departure from New York, three Americans died when the U.S. tanker *Gulflight* was severely damaged by a U-boat's torpedo, apparently a case of mistaken identity. Americans were shocked. The influential *New York Times*

When the Lusitania sank, President Woodrow Wilson (right and below with his cabinet) had not yet responded to the German torpedoing the week before of the American tanker Gulflight (far right) with the loss of three lives.

called the attack a flagrant "violation of our rights." But Wilson did not declare war. In fact he had not even sent a note of protest about the incident when, a week later, Walther Schwieger fired the fatal torpedo at the *Lusitania*.

When the big Cunarder went down, Berlin apologized to the U.S., expressing its "deepest sympathy" at the loss of American lives. At the same time, they pointed out that the responsibility for the tragedy rested with the British government which, "through its plan of starving the civilian population," had forced Germany into taking retaliatory measures.

A few days later Wilson responded. In terms that must have been an echo of notes written to recalcitrant students during his time as a college teacher, he told the Germans that they had been warned of the consequences of their actions but had gone ahead anyway. He reminded them of his "strict accountability" missive

of February 10, 1915 (adding, incorrectly, that he had declared the rights of "American citizens bound on lawful errands as passengers of merchant ships of belligerent nationality" to be inviolate). The German diplomats who first read the note must have thought something earthshaking was coming. But at this point Wilson stepped back from the brink. He complained about the "practical impossibility" of submarines being used humanely, apparently implying that all would be forgiven if Germany stopped using U-boats. Like many people of that time, the president could accept the notion of merchantmen being stopped and searched (and sunk if they were found to be carrying contraband), but torpedoing without warning simply could not be tolerated.

He concluded his note by declaring that he expected Germany to disavow the sinking and to take "immediate steps" to prevent such a thing from ever

happening again. What would "immediate steps" mean? A break in diplomatic relations seemed to be in Wilson's mind, but he didn't spell it out.

The Germans quickly concluded that Wilson's note was as much for domestic consumption as for Berlin's. They were correct. Wilson, the consummate politician, had shrewdly gauged the nation's mood. Americans wanted the Germans to know that they had overstepped the bounds of civilized behavior, but few wanted to go to war over it. The British tended to think of Americans as transplanted Britons, all of them sympathetic to Britain's aspirations. It was a serious misconception. Vast numbers of Americans felt not the slightest kinship with the British. Many, particularly those of Irish descent, were actively anti-British. So, it may be assumed, was the nearly ten percent of the population with German ancestors.

The exchange of notes continued, with Berlin

repeatedly complaining (not unreasonably) that Wilson was treating the belligerents quite differently, ignoring such flagrant illegalities as the British using neutral — including American — colors to avoid interception. Moreover, Berlin pointed out, the *Lusitania* was no ordinary passenger liner but an auxiliary cruiser, "constructed with government funds" and "included in the navy list."

The communications, so icily polite in the manner of all diplomatic exchanges, caused Wilson more than a few problems at home. William Jennings Bryan, the ardently pacifistic secretary of state, thought Wilson was leading the U.S. into war by accusing and provoking Germany. He resigned, whereupon the more vociferous supporters of the Allied cause called him a coward, a "white-livered scoundrel," and a friend of the kaiser's. Robert Lansing took over as secretary of state. He was less statesmanlike than Bryan but he brought to the post an unblemished record of Hun-hating.

In Germany the sinking was reported as a triumph of the country's naval might. The *Lusitania* was an "armed cruiser" carrying munitions and other war supplies and was therefore a legitimate target, readers were told. Most editorials expressed amazement that civilians, particularly Americans, would persist in traveling with the "profit-hungry" Cunard company after the warning so sportingly provided by the German embassy. As the *Kölnische Volkszeitung* pointed out: "The English wish to abandon the German people to death by starvation. We are more humane. We simply sank an English ship with passengers who, at their own risk and responsibility, entered the zone of operations."

~

THE STORY SOON SLIPPED FROM THE HEADLINES. THE war provided an endless supply of new tragedies: the Dardanelles disaster, poison gas, the bombing of civilians, starvation, the slaughter at Verdun, the Somme and Passchendaele.

Queenstown, 7. Mai 1915.
Der Cunarddampfer "Lusitania" ist torpediert worden und gesunken.

But the echoes of the *Lusitania* kept reverberating. The questions wouldn't go away. Why did the ship sail right into a U-boat's path? And why so slowly? Why were no escorts ready to see her safely into Liverpool? Why did the ship so widely publicized as unsinkable go to the bottom so rapidly? Why was the crew apparently so ill-prepared for the emergency? Why were the passengers not instructed about which lifeboats they were to use or even how to put on their life belts? Why did Captain Turner sail so close to land? Why did he not zigzag to spoil the aim of the U-boat?

⚓

THE FIRST OFFICIAL INQUIRY BEGAN THE DAY AFTER the sinking. Five victims had been brought ashore at Kinsale, a small fishing village about fifteen miles from Queenstown. The local coroner, John J. Horgan, did not lose a moment convening a jury of shopkeepers and fishermen. Apparently relishing the limelight

ZEICHNET KRIEGS-ANLEIHE FÜR U-BOOTE GEGEN ENGLAND

To the Germans the Lusitania *(left) was a munitions-carrying merchant cruiser caught in a war zone (above). (Right) Captain Turner after the sinking.*

into which he and his tiny community had been thrust, he said the proceedings had been called to investigate an "inhuman crime" in which two torpedoes, the second even more powerful than the first, were used to sink the passenger liner *Lusitania*.

The first witness to be called was District Inspector Wainsborough, who described how the naval patrol vessel *Heron* had anchored in Kinsale harbor the previous evening. On board were five bodies, victims of the *Lusitania* disaster, plus eleven survivors. In fact, said Wainsborough, it was because one of the survivors, a Mrs. Julia Sullivan, needed medical attention that the skipper decided to land at Kinsale rather than Queenstown. With the frosty courtesy common to law courts, Horgan expressed the hope that Mrs. Sullivan was progressing satisfactorily. Wainsborough said she was.

Horgan adjourned the inquest until Monday.

⚓

CAPTAIN WILLIAM TURNER CAME TO the stand. He was a pathetic figure, stooped and obviously not yet fully recovered from his ordeal. His borrowed uniform was a size or two too large; it made him look as if he had shrunk.

Horgan thanked Turner for appearing at the inquiry and assured him that the questions would be kept to a minimum.

Responding to Horgan's questions, Turner declared that he was aware that threats had been made against his ship in New York. He stated that the *Lusitania* was not armed. He admitted that he had received warnings about the presence of submarines off the Irish coast. According to his testimony, he was on the bridge when the torpedo struck and remained there until he was swept off by the sea when the *Lusitania* sank.

He was of the (mistaken) opinion that Schwieger's missile had hit his ship between "the fourth and third funnels." Moments later, another explosion, even more powerful than the first, rocked the ship.

Why, Turner was asked, did he reduce his speed as he neared Ireland? The captain explained that thick fog had been experienced during the morning. When the skies began to clear, he decided to sail straight into Liverpool without stopping to pick up a pilot. This required a steady speed of eighteen knots. Under the circumstances, he asserted, it was the most prudent course of action. Missing the tide and taking on a pilot would have meant stopping, and stationary targets were particularly vulnerable to U-boat attack. None of the jury questioned his statement. Interestingly, one member did ask Turner if he had been zigzagging at the time of the attack. He said no.

None of the jury asked why not.

But they did ask about the unsuccessful attempts to launch lifeboats. Turner explained that the ship's list made the procedure extremely difficult and hazardous, even though every effort had been made, and the crew had obeyed his orders diligently. There was no panic among the passengers, he declared. The jury did not ask if there was panic among the crew.

According to Turner, the Cunard company had not requested an escort from the Admiralty despite all the glib assurances in New York. In fact, even if Cunard had demanded an escort for the *Lusitania*, it's doubtful that the Admiralty could have obliged. The Royal Navy was hard pressed to meet its naval obligations. It had no escort ships available for passenger liners on normal civilian journeys. And, as was known, had the *Lusitania* been escorted by a naval vessel, she would have become part of a naval unit and therefore a legitimate target for U-boats, according to maritime law.

One juror asked about the ship's bulkhead doors. Were they closed? Turner said yes. Were the passengers all provided with life belts? Yes again. No one asked if the passengers had received any instructions on how to put the life belts on or how to adjust them to make

In June 1915, the British Board of Trade launched its official inquiry at Westminster Hall. Heading it was Lord Mersey, the same judge who had conducted the official investigation into the loss of the Titanic.

inquiry to blame each other for the tragedy, but Mersey wouldn't have it. The inquiry had been organized to tell the world who was responsible for "the foulest crime ever committed," and he didn't want the issue clouded by comparatively unimportant disagreements between Cunard and the Admiralty.

Whatever Lord Mersey privately thought of Captain Turner and his handling of the *Lusitania* before and during the emergency, he made sure that the proceedings in the somber surroundings of Central Hall, Westminster, resulted in no criticism of the veteran sailor. As at Kinsale, there was to be only one guilty party: Germany.

Once again Turner was a key witness. And,

however skilled the legal help appointed, they uncovered little more of the story than did the coroner's inquest. Turner explained that the *Lusitania*'s speed was only eighteen knots because of the fog and his plan to sail right into Liverpool with the tide. And, no, he wasn't really worried about submarines. His speed was adequate and sailing straight through was safer than stopping to pick up a pilot.

Turner did, however, have some difficulty responding to questions about his failure to zigzag. He was aware of the order that ships should zigzag in waters where U-boats were believed to be lurking. But, he admitted apologetically, he had misinterpreted the Admiralty's instructions. He was under the impression that zigzagging was supposed to start when he saw a U-boat, not before.

Why, Carson asked him, had he steered so close to the Old Head of Kinsale, when the Admiralty advised all ships to stay in midchannel?

Turner explained that he wanted to take a four-point navigational bearing on the headland. The ship had been in thick fog for several hours. When conditions improved and land was in sight, he wished to determine his exact position. He knew approximately where he was, he declared, but not precisely.

Turner's testimony reinforced the image of the

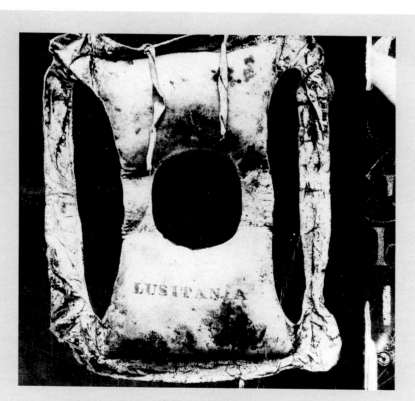

MEMENTO OF A TRAGEDY

Five years after the *Lusitania* went down, this life jacket from the ship was fished from the Delaware River at Philadelphia. The jacket must have been carried south by the current to Africa before washing west and then bobbing its way up the east coast of the U.S. — a journey of many thousands of miles.

crusty captain, set in his ways and reluctant to change for anything as trivial as a world war. He seemed to find nothing curious about sailing in a perfectly straight line beside a coast known to be infested with U-boats. He evidently believed it preferable to slow down and sail close to the many headlands — favorite spots for lurking submarines — than to run the risk of arriving at Liverpool ahead of schedule.

The *Lusitania* was only about a dozen miles off the Old Head when Schwieger's torpedo struck her. Carson asked whether Turner had received the Admiralty's instructions about sailing in midchannel. Turner said he had. Carson seemed puzzled. Did Turner suggest that when torpedoed he was sailing in midchannel?

"It is practically what I call midchannel," Turner responded awkwardly. Later he changed his story somewhat, stating that he stayed out of the *middle* of the channel because he believed a submarine to be lurking there.

Cunard officials must have groaned inwardly as question succeeded question. When asked about the performance of his crew after the torpedo attack, Turner said they did a competent job, although he admitted that they experienced great difficulty in launching the lifeboats because of a list of about fifteen degrees, which rapidly grew worse. The crew should have been more proficient at handling the lifeboats, Turner admitted, but he made no apologies for that fact; it was the same on all ships in wartime, he explained. Crews had to be made up of the men available, no matter what their experience, or lack of it. He admitted that the crew needed a great deal more practice with the boats. No one asked why, during the days before the torpedoing, he failed to give the crew the practice they needed, or even to institute proper lifeboat drills for crew and passengers.

Carson asked Turner whether his ship was armed or unarmed.

"Unarmed," responded Turner without hesitation.

"Had she any weapons of offence or defence against the enemy at all?"

"No."

❧

ALFRED BOOTH, THE CHAIRMAN OF CUNARD, TESTIFIED at the inquiry, stating without apology that it had been a company decision to run the *Lusitania* at "three-fourths boiler power." This, he declared, resulted in a reduction of speed from an average of about 24 knots to some 21 knots. Cunard's directors, he added, were of the opinion that "the difference between 21 and 24 knots was not material so far as avoiding submarines was concerned."

The inquiry ended. It placed the entire burden of guilt on Germany, while absolving Cunard and the Royal Navy of any blame. Perhaps such an inquiry, held in wartime, couldn't have had any other result. Whole-hearted condemnation of Captain Turner, Cunard or the

THE *LUSITANIA* AMBULANCES

One lasting legacy of the disaster were the so-called *Lusitania* ambulances. Capitalizing on the nationalistic fervor surrounding the sinking, Cunard donated a pair of ambulances for war service. Dedicated by Lady Booth, wife of Cunard's chairman, in a service outside the Liverpool Cunard office, the ambulances saw service in France.

Royal Navy would have been less than appropriate. It might even have been considered treasonable in those emotionally overheated times. But the inquiry did little to assuage the anger of those who had lost loved ones or valuable property. And it failed to answer some of the most contentious of questions. Had some of the crew behaved poorly when disaster struck? Was the captain guilty of gross negligence in his handling of his ship? Should the Royal Navy have done more? Was the *Lusitania* carrying explosives? In many people's minds the inquiry raised more questions than it answered. But no matter. Walther Schwieger and the *U-20*'s crew, and indeed the entire German nation and the Central Powers, were to be the only guilty parties. They sent the fatal torpedo into the passenger ship's unprotected side. They caused the deaths of over a thousand innocents.

But was it all quite so simple? The British government had proudly placed the *Lusitania* and *Mauretania* on the navy list as auxiliary cruisers, and had taken to equipping merchant ships with concealed weapons. These two facts would have made Schwieger wary of revealing himself before firing his torpedo. Such details, however, were conveniently ignored.

TWO YEARS AFTER THE SINKING, THIRTY-THREE OF THE witnesses from the Mersey inquiry appeared before a commissioner of oaths in London. Their evidence was required for an inquiry to be held in New York to hear nearly seventy actions by individuals and groups. Most of the actions involved claims for compensatory damages against Cunard.

The case was heard by Judge Julius M. Mayer, the former attorney general for the state of New York. By the time the case came to court, innumerable articles and several books had been written about the *Lusitania* tragedy, and one other event of great significance had taken place: the United States had gone to war with Germany. Thus the Mayer inquiry was just as hamstrung by security restrictions as the Mersey inquiry had been. Perhaps the most significant thing about the New York hearing is that the attorneys for the

complainants made no mention of guns, high explosives or troops in their brief — points that the Germans had complained about so vociferously. The fact is, after examining the evidence, the documents and earlier oral testimony, they could find nothing to support the theories they would have been delighted to use in the presentation of their case.

CAPTAIN TURNER HAD BEEN ONE OF THE KEY WITNESSES to appear in London. This time his evidence was submitted to Judge Mayer in written form.

Turner's testimony now bore the fruits of two years of polishing and editing, no doubt with the invaluable assistance of the Cunard legal counsel, Butler Aspinall. He had little new to tell the American judge. His ship had carried no guns or high explosives; he used the term "safety cartridges" when referring to the ammunition stowed in the hold. He repeated what he had already said about the speed he was making when the *U-20*'s torpedo struck home. He admitted that he could have ordered the six unused boilers activated — the ship then could have delivered its maximum speed of about twenty-five knots — although it would have taken some hours to build up the pressure. He felt eighteen knots were satisfactory under the circumstances.

He was also still of the opinion that to all intents and purposes he was obeying Admiralty instructions and sailing "midchannel," even though he agreed that he was little more than a dozen miles from the coast. On the question of zigzagging, Turner had had an opportunity to hone his story about believing that the Admiralty directive involved zigzagging only after sighting a submarine. In his testimony, Turner classified the Admiralty instructions as mere "suggestions."

JUDGE MAYER RENDERED HIS DECISION IN AUGUST 1918. War fervor still gripped the Allied nations, and Mayer's decision reflected that fact, disappointing only those of his countrymen who had liability cases against Cunard. Neither the steamship company nor Captain

Turner were to blame, ruled Mayer. He declared the ship and its lifeboats to be in "excellent order," although many survivors disagreed with him. Boat drills? They were "sufficient and proficient," according to his ruling, and no charge of negligence and incompetence by the crew could be sustained. Mayer disregarded the testimony of one witness who claimed to have seen a crew member releasing a rope prematurely and dumping a boatload of passengers into the sea, and that of another who saw one lifeboat leaving the ship full of sailors. As far as Judge Mayer was concerned, the blame for the whole sorry business, one of the "most indefensible acts of modern times," belonged in only one place: on the doorstep of Imperial Germany. He added that the attack "was deliberately and long contemplated." The purpose of sinking the *Lusitania* had been simply to destroy lives and property. In other words, there was no tactical purpose in sinking the liner. It was spite, pure and simple, according to Mayer, an opinion shared by the vast majority of those in the Allied camp.

So ended the official inquiries into the sinking of the *Lusitania*.

Turner also had an opportunity to tell his story directly to a wide audience in November 1915. Cunard had given him command of a ten-thousand-ton freighter, the *Ultonia*, and he sailed her from France to Quebec City. While there, he went to New York to spend a few days with an old friend, and during his stay he granted an interview to the *New York Times*. He told the reporter that he had seen the advertisement placed by the German embassy (although pro-German activists were probably responsible). He read it, he said, but he never believed such a dreadful thing would ever take place. Nevertheless, he hastened to add, he made sure that the ship was prepared for any emergency.

Turner admitted that many members of his crew were less experienced than he would have liked. "The old-fashioned able seaman who could knot, reef, splice or steer disappeared with the sailing ships," he said. He maintained, however, that all hands were well drilled in their emergency duties: "I am satisfied that every precaution was taken and that nothing was left undone that might have helped to save lives that day." At 5:00 P.M. on the evening before the sinking, lifeboats were swung out and he ordered all bulkhead doors

Judge Julius M. Mayer shown aboard the liner Olympic, *sister of the* Titanic.

closed. "No matter what we had done or what speed the *Lusitania* had been going, the submarines would have got her, as they had planned on it, by getting the angles on the course approaching the Irish coast and were just waiting to blow her up with all on board." Turner believed that two or possibly three U-boats were involved. There was no panic among passengers, he said, "until steerage passengers started to scream and rush about." Turner looked thinner since the sinking, reported the paper, and his hair was grayer.

The following year Turner took over command of a fourteen-thousand-ton Cunarder, the troop carrier *Ivernia*. Off Cape Matapan on New Year's Day, 1917, the *Ivernia* was torpedoed. Although thirty-six lost their lives, Turner again survived.

The PROPAGANDA WAR

Several survivors of the sinking had clear and intensely painful memories of struggling in the frigid water while the

A German illustration (above) shows a sinking Lusitania *armed with small gun turrets. In contrast, this Allied cartoon (left) depicts the kaiser, draped in a Teutonic Jolly Roger, standing beside the warning placed in the American newspapers. As propaganda, the Germans struck a medal ridiculing Cunard's "callous" decision to carry passengers on a "blockade runner." Seizing on it as proof of German barbarism, the British stamped out thousands of copies (below) and used it on posters (right).*

FAC-SIMILE OF MEDAL STRU
TO COMMEMORATE
Translation of wordi
BUSINESS ABOVE EVERYTHING NO
CUNARD LINE—CUNARD-BOOKING GRE
OFFICE—SUBMARINE DANGER SIN

crew of the *U-20* clustered on the deck and conning tower, jeering, pointing, laughing, enjoying the spectacle.

In fact, the *U-20* didn't surface after it torpedoed the *Lusitania*. What those survivors remembered was a cartoon, published shortly after the tragedy, depicting precisely the scene that they recalled so vividly. Perhaps it wasn't surprising. The loss of the famous ship generated an immense amount of publicity. In many people's minds it

WE FORGET

The Sinking of the Lusitania.
May 7th 1915.

became difficult to separate this propaganda from the sinking itself. And the governments involved did their utmost to fan the fires of controversy.

British military authorities also noted the effect the sinking had on recruiting. Like advertising executives studying marketing campaigns, senior officers paid close attention to the themes that "paid off" at the recruiting centers. Soon posters everywhere depicted horrific scenes of the mighty Cunarder going down while hapless passengers struggled in the chilly water. "Take up the Sword of Justice" commanded one poster as the *Lusitania* took her last dive in the background. "Remember the *Lusitania*" became the same kind of rallying cry for the British as "Remember the Alamo" had once been for the Americans.

Cartoonists liked to depict Germans either as slavering, mindless beasts killing anyone who happened to get in their

way, or as wickedly devious plotters forever cooking up some nastiness for the rest of the world. In such cartoons, Kaiser Wilhelm sometimes looked like a villain in a Victorian melodrama, complete with black cape and top hat; sometimes he became a Hun warrior with a spiked helmet and matching mustache.

For their part, German cartoonists characterized John Bull as an obese bully boy, King George as a dithering idiot, and Uncle Sam as a gangling hillbilly. It was all standard treatment in the propaganda war. "They" were ruthless and merciless yet at the same time not too bright. By contrast, "our" soldiers were

invariably cheerful with just the right touch of irreverence. The propaganda chiefs made no secret of their aims: to encourage hatred of the other side, to preserve the friendship of the allies, to generate the sympathy of neutrals and, whenever possible, to demoralize the enemy.

The *Lusitania* sinking was

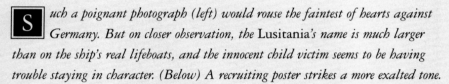

S uch a poignant photograph (left) would rouse the faintest of hearts against Germany. But on closer observation, the Lusitania's *name is much larger than on the ship's real lifeboats, and the innocent child victim seems to be having trouble staying in character. (Below) A recruiting poster strikes a more exalted tone.*

TAKE UP THE SWORD OF JUSTICE

IRISHMEN
AVENGE THE LUSITANIA

JOIN AN IRISH REGIMENT
TO-DAY.

ISSUED BY THE CENTRAL COUNCIL FOR THE ORGANISATION OF RECRUITING IN IRELAND.   John Shuley & Co. Dublin.   Wt. P. 110—7,500   5 15

British recruiting officers noted an increase in enlistments after the Lusitania sinking and decided to capitalize on it further (left). After they entered the war, the Americans also used it for recruiting (opposite top), and to sell bonds (opposite middle). Corpulent Germans gloat over their atrocity (opposite bottom), although the guilty submarine is misidentified as U-24.

—From La Revue Hebdominaire, Paris.

excellent grist for the Allied propaganda mill. It had all the elements: a cruel enemy; innocent, unarmed victims; the involvement of lots of friendly Yanks; and, perhaps above all, *dimension*. Like the ship itself, the story captured the imagination. So the authorities issued press releases, sent out copies of photographs, wrote scripts for slide shows and articles for magazines. It was a highly successful effort and undoubtedly did far more to generate support for the Allied cause than a thousand political speeches. Photographs of victims and detailed sketches of the sinking ship filled the newspapers and magazines across Britain. "Snatched from the fury of the Germans," read the caption beneath a photograph of survivors who reached dry land. "For victims of Germany's greatest piracy," said another showing cartloads of empty coffins being brought into Queenstown.

The fact was, of course, that the Germans were being blockaded by the Royal Navy; most believed (correctly) that the British had no compunction about starving them to death — men, women and children — if that was what it would take to win. The majority of Germans saw the *Lusitania* affair as an heroic attack on an "armed

auxiliary cruiser," a brilliant blow against a merciless enemy who should be heartily condemned for his conduct.

There can be no doubt, however, that the *Lusitania* sinking did irreparable harm to Germany's propaganda efforts in the United States. The German ambassador to Washington admitted to his superiors that the *Lusitania* incident had caused the complete collapse of his staff's efforts to enhance his nation's image in America. Although millions of pro-German citizens lived in the United States, most quickly sensed that the country as a whole sympathized with the British.

As the war years rolled on, the *Lusitania* story continued to surface from time to time. Perhaps its most bizarre manifestation was a film, *The Kaiser, the Beast of Berlin*. In this 1918 concoction of Jewel Productions, the commander of the *U-20*, Walther Schwieger, is decorated by the kaiser for sinking the *Lusitania*; then, presumably weighed down by guilt, goes mad and commits suicide. A cinema in Omaha, Nebraska, showed the film with great success. A sign on the door said All Pro-Germans Admitted Free.

According to the proprietor, no patrons availed themselves of this generous offer.

Chapter Seven

Exploring the *Lusitania*

(Above) Jason *is recovered after a night dive.*
(Right) The submarine Delta *illuminates the*
Lusitania's *name, still visible on her bow.*

W HEN IT CAME TO the exploration of the wreck of the *Lusitania*, we had a big advantage. We didn't have to waste time searching for the ship, as was necessary with the *Titanic* or the *Bismarck* or our other expeditions. Local fisherman knew the precise location, having caught countless nets on her over the years, so our command ship, the *Northern Horizon*, took up station directly over the remains of the Cunarder. From there the Irish coast looks tantalizingly close, apparently within reach of a strong swimmer. But any of the passengers or crew of the *Lusitania* who attempted the journey soon found out how far it really was.

We had little to say to each other as we went into the darkened *Jason* control van mounted on the deck of the *Northern Horizon*. In that tiny room display screens and control panels had priority over mere humans. We squeezed ourselves into whatever spaces we could find and prepared for the great adventure. Step number one was to complete a sonar reconnaissance of the wreck. From our preliminary investigations we knew that she was on her starboard side, minus her funnels and most of her superstructure.

We soon learned that the *Lusitania* lay along a bearing of about 230 degrees, or southwest to northeast. We began our series of runs, gradually creating an outline of the wreck from the sonar echoes. The great hull had been torn open during the sinking, the fracture occurring between the third and fourth funnels. The bent hull now forms a shape like a gigantic boomerang on the seabed. The break had occurred in about the same general area as that on the *Titanic*, around where the huge dining room and first-class lounge had been located. The great open areas of such rooms on these ships were never meant for such stress. Most of the hull seemed to be smooth, but the sonar returns from the superstructure painted a chaotic picture of destruction and confusion.

Tucked away on the command ship was our unique fleet of vehicles: *Delta*, our minisubmarine; *Jason*, our 3,000 lb. remotely operated vehicle; *Medea*, a small robot vehicle; and little *Homer*, borrowed from the Harbor

Our control center aboard Northern Horizon *was a converted ship container outfitted with an array of computers and television monitors (right). Another container (left) had stored our submarine*

Delta *and its spare parts. Much of the remote exploration would be done by* Jason *(left). We also relied on our smaller vehicle,* Homer *(above, on the left)*

Branch Oceanographic Institution. This collection of manned and unmanned vehicles provided us with the means to examine the wreck at close quarters and produce excellent-quality photographs of our findings.

Once the sonar mapping had been completed, it was time to dispatch *Jason* on a reconnaissance of the site. With Martin Bowen handling the controls in our command center, *Jason*, followed by *Medea*, slipped into a choppy sea and began the journey to the bottom. Huddled in our cramped seats, we watched the action on the TV screens as the robot vehicle slid down into the darkness. Schools of fish brushed past, apparently unafraid of the mechanical intruder in their midst. Then at last we glimpsed the great liner.

None of us said a word. The *Lusitania* was the technological wonder of her age, as astonishing to the Edwardian era as the Stealth Bomber is in our time. She was the first liner to use the huge turbines that are now the standard form of power for big ships, and she was the first to incorporate power-assisted controls and

such luxuries as electric elevators between decks. The *Lusitania* was the stuff of legend, her name ranking high on any list of maritime immortals. And here she was, close enough, it seemed, to touch.

The legend has been humbled. She lies broken and battered, most of her superstructure gone, many of her portside doors thrown wide open, a sorry shadow of her former self. No longer is she the haughty "floating palace" patronized by the titled and the fabulously wealthy of Europe and America; no longer is she the proud holder of the Blue Riband for the fastest crossing of the Atlantic. As well, over the past eighty years, various diving expeditions have stripped her of much of her remaining beauty. Most recently a lawsuit has been filed with the state of Virginia between the *Lusitania*'s declared owner Gregg Bemis and a group of divers who removed material from the ship in the summer of 1994. As I have said repeatedly in the past, although I believe in unlimited access to historic ships like the *Lusitania*, I am opposed to the taking of artifacts. These ships should be left intact, both as memorials and as archaeological sites of interest to future generations.

Yet even now she possesses a certain dignity. Her steelwork is surprisingly clean, with little encrustation and marine growth; her hull retains a lot of its coat of antifouling paint, which looks remarkably fresh after eighty years on the seabed. Many portholes seem as good as new, with their glass unbroken.

We encountered one potential danger. Parts of the hull were shrouded in nylon fishing nets that had snagged on the wreck. I'd learned from bitter experience to steer well clear of such nets in remotely controlled vehicles.

I'm sure that explorers who unearth ancient works of art must feel much the same as we did as we sat transfixed in that cramped room on the deck of the *Northern Horizon*. We had found a great treasure, a marvel from another time. But sadness tinged our excitement; our thoughts inevitably turned to the passengers and crew who died in the sinking, innocent victims of war.

As Martin Bowen pilots Jason*, I check a detail of the wreckage against an old photograph of the* Lusitania.

Jason scurried away on its visual survey, tirelessly exploring, traveling back and forth over the acres of steel, studying every square inch of the ship. High-frequency sonar provided us with a computerized, color-coded, three-dimensional diagram of the wreck, an invaluable guide for our investigation. On the diagram we were able to superimpose a 3-D image of the great ship in her prime and thus see at a glance the areas that had been most affected by the sinking.

The *Lusitania* has become a playground for thousands of fish that dart around her twisted decks, slipping in and out of her portholes and slinking around her long-silent engine rooms, cabins and lounges.

The wreck appears curiously deflated, for her decks have collapsed and her insides are squashed and crumpled. A nightmarish hall-of-mirrors look permeates those silent corridors and cabins, once so luxuriously appointed and scrupulously maintained. They have become grotesque caricatures of their elegant former selves. The metalwork, the decks, the walls have folded and twisted under the crushing burden of gravity, and the ship's beam has shrunk to about forty feet from the original eighty-eight. Her funnels are missing, their thin steel now totally rusted away. In an eerie way the magnificent *Lusitania* seems to be reverting to her youth, shedding those parts added after she was launched on a bright spring day in June 1906.

It was a thrill to see her name under *Jason's* lights. The brass letters were painted over for security reasons early in the war. Since then corrosion has destroyed the fasteners that held them in place. They have fallen off and vanished in the sand and silt on the ocean bed, but their outlines are still visible. No archaeologist deciphering prehistoric hieroglyphics in some long-undiscovered cave could have been more excited than we were.

Our first attempts to maneuver *Jason* close to the wreck were frustrated by a strong current on the seabed. Then our lights attracted countless pollack that swarmed past, blocking the wreck from our view. We had to wait until they lost interest in us and moved away. At last we were able to proceed with our mission.

We spotted an enormous fracture in the hull where the steel plates had separated. The rivet holes were empty, the rivets themselves no doubt falling out as the

Chapter Eight

LUSITANIA
Then
and Now

The Lusitania *today lies on her starboard side almost three hundred feet down. Although time has been hard on her, it is still possible to find connections between the wreck and the Blue Riband–winning pride of the Cunard line. (Left) The outline of the ship's name is still visible on the bow, and by combining numerous photographs, it is possible to spell it in full (below). (Bottom) The* Lusitania's *name as it originally appeared.*

The Bow

The bow bent upward when the ship hit the bottom, making this one of the few areas of the ship where it is possible to see the starboard side (below left). (Left) Delta moves in to explore the port bow. (Below) The tip of the bow as it looked in *Lusitania's* prime. Both of the ship's anchors are visible here. Today only the starboard anchor (right) is still attached to

the ship. (This picture has been righted for ease of recognition.) (Overleaf) Delta explores the starboard bow.

The Foredeck

On the forward deck among the fishing nets and decay
it is possible to pick out details visible in this period
picture (opposite, bottom right). Among these are a wheel
similar to the windlass brake (opposite, top) and these
bollards (opposite, bottom left), which still have a rope
wrapped around them. In the jumble of wreckage nearer
the bow are this small crane (above) and a section of
chain (right), which may have been used to moor the
ship to the Cunard buoy at Liverpool.

(Right) The Lusitania's triple-chime whistle was mounted on the foremost funnel and was almost three feet high. Today it lies in the sand near the liner (above). The steam pipes, which also lie on the bottom, (opposite bottom) were once attached to one of the Lusitania's funnels like the one that is visible here.

Aft of the bridge was an area called the "top of house," which was lined with the Lusitania's distinctive vents (above). Although it has lost its lid, this vent (top right) is still recognizable when compared with one from eighty years ago. (Right) This mosaic-tile floor was found in the vestibule in first class that passengers entered off the boat deck.

The Water Tanks

Immediately behind the first funnel, the Lusitania *carried three large water tanks (below). These are still in place on the deck and readily recognizable (left and bottom).*

Aboard Lusitania, only first-class baths were equipped with showers. This one now sits amid scattered debris outside the wreck. (Right) How the shower looked when installed. (Opposite top) This window, with its filigreed detail, once graced the rooms located along Lusitania's boat deck (middle right). (Opposite middle) This simpler window and the electrical light fixture beside it were found on the ship's covered promenade deck (far right).

This lifeboat davit is one of only three that are still attached to the **Lusitania**. It has snagged some of the nylon fishing net that we found on so much of the wreck. (Left) The same davit as it was in 1915.

(Right) This door in the side of the ship was used for passenger entry. (Below) One of these same doors today, thrown wide open. How so heavy a door came to be opened is a mystery. (Overleaf) Delta *explores the massive break in the* Lusitania's *side.*

(Right) Inside the large crack in the side of the Lusitania. *a row of double rivets is visible. These match a double row on the side of similar boilers shown in the old photograph (below). This told us we were looking into one of the*

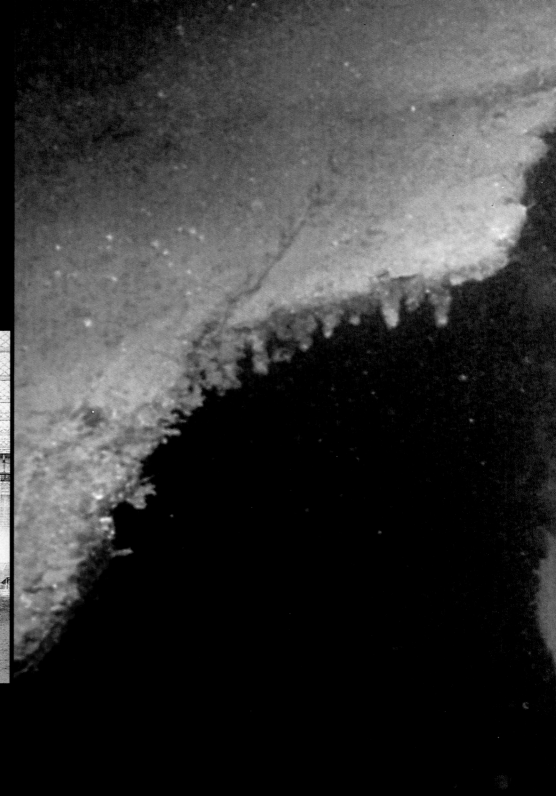

Lusitania's *boiler rooms. specifically number four. which had been shut down as an economy measure and was not in use on her final voyage.*

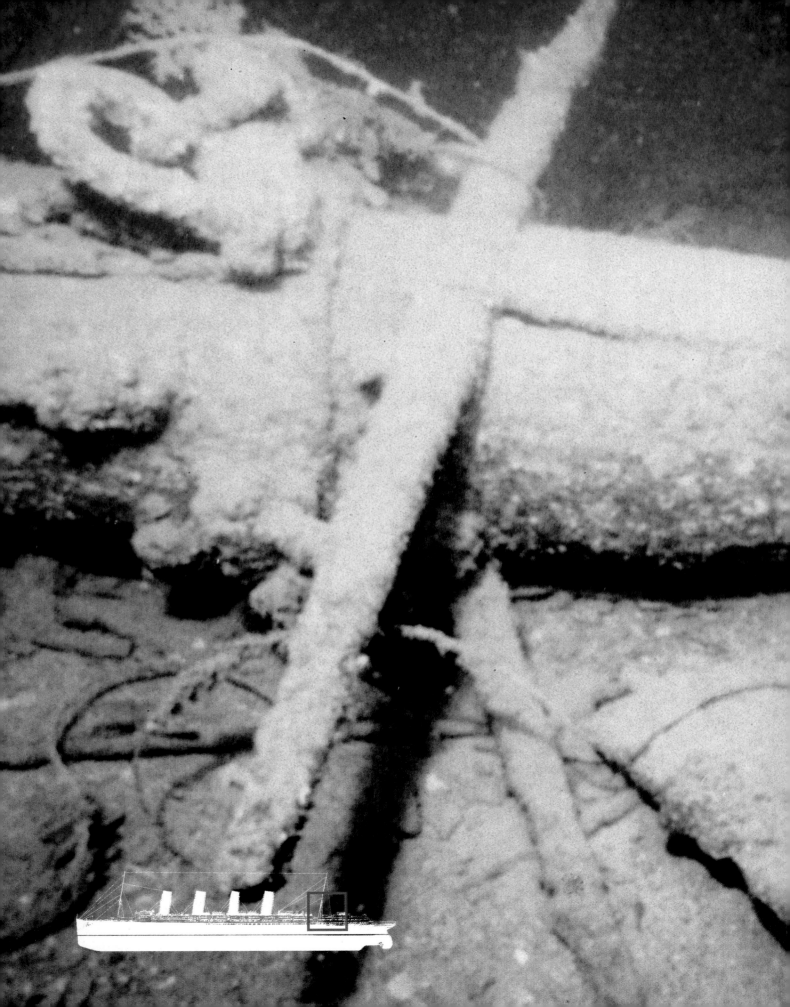

(Left) The ship's mainmast, lying in the wreckage, and (right) as it looked in place. (Below) Fish swim through one of the skylights from atop the

aft deckhouse that was once home to many of the second-class public rooms. (Right) The skylight as it looked in 1915.

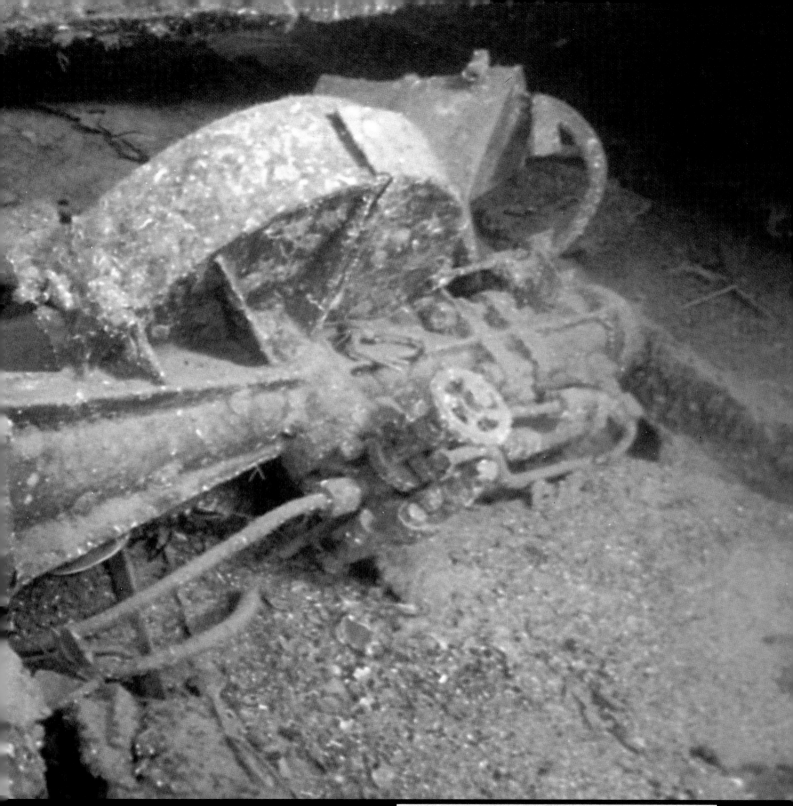

Aft Docking Bridge

Located on the aft boat deck (right), the docking bridge had its own controls to help guide the ship into its berth in port. Today it has been torn right off the ship (left), and the telemotor that held the docking bridge's wheel now lies on its side (above).

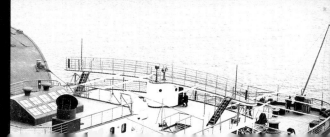

Props and Rudder

(Top) This bossing once held one of the Lusitania's port propellers before it was removed by salvagers. (Above) The Lusitania's rudder is still in place, but the bottom has been broken off. (Left) The same propeller and the rudder as they looked in place. (Right) One of the propellers today, in a Welsh scrapyard.

Engine Room

(Left) Because the superstructure has slid away over the years, it is possible to look right into the engine room. It is badly battered, but there are features that make it recognizable — notably the metal girder running across the room and the remains of the metal catwalk (above).

Trapped on the *Lusitania*

In August 1993, artist Ken Marschall and historian Eric Sauder went down to explore the wreck aboard the versatile minisubmarine *Delta*. The passengers had to kneel in the confined space, peering out through the portholes. Chris Ijames, a highly experienced pilot, handled the controls. *Delta* had some two thousand dives to its credit, and had never run into any problems, but on this day things went wrong. Attempting to ride the sub over the spiderweb of nets that cling to the *Lusitania*, Chris felt an ominous tug. The nets had caught *Delta*, and they held it fast. Chris tried every maneuver to pull his craft free. But the net wouldn't let go. Fortunately, the sub's rear rudder and propeller had been made jettisonable for just such an emergency. After stowing various heavy items aft, Chris carefully removed the fasteners holding the assembly in position. Instantly *Delta* shifted, and to the relief of its occupants, it rose at a brisk pace.

On the way to the surface, Eric recalls that he felt as if the sub would "shoot out of the water like a missile." It didn't. "Chris released air as we rose, slowing our rate of ascent dramatically. Thousands of tiny bubbles made a trickling sound past our ports."

Luckily for our expedition, *Delta* was equipped with a replacement tail. A few days later, with her new rudder and propeller assembly in place, she dived on the *Lusitania* and recovered her missing aft section. Eric Sauder kept this as a memento of his nerve-racking adventure.

Probably the most poignant sights on the Lusitania *are those with the strongest human connections. One can easily imagine that (top) people once ate off these plates, (above) a woman's foot once slipped into this shoe and (below) excited passengers once leaned on this railing to catch their first glimpse of New York.*

Chapter Nine

What Sank the *Lusitania?*

O NCE WE HAD INVESTIGATED the wreck of the *Lusitania*, it was time to try to draw some conclusions. What had sunk the great ship?

The *Lusitania* disaster is widely remembered as "the sinking that brought America into the war." Indeed, over the years there have been charges that the British engineered the whole thing to foment trouble between the United States and Germany. Winston Churchill, then First Lord of the Admiralty, is usually the man blamed.

Such theories received wide circulation during the war via several pro-German newspapers and magazines in America. A congressman of the time, Richmond Hobson, made no secret of his belief that the British had arranged to have the *Lusitania* sunk (although few took much notice of him). Oswald Flamm, a German privy councillor, even claimed that the devilish English plotters had persuaded someone to set off a bomb moments after the torpedo to make sure that the ship would sink rapidly. Proponents of such theories point to Captain Turner's failure to take any evasive action off the coast of Ireland. They apparently believed that Turner agreed to steam in a perfectly straight line so that his ship would be as easy a target as possible for the waiting Schwieger.

Winston Churchill was accused of allowing the sinking. (Right) Homer probes under the Lusitania's *keel.*

The kaiser himself seemed to support the notion. A year after the sinking, he told the U.S. ambassador, James W. Gerard, that the British government "made the *Lusitania* go slowly in English waters so that the Germans could torpedo it and so bring on trouble."

So was the sinking part of a Machiavellian British plot to unite the neutral nations of the world, including the United States, in an anti-German alliance? It's an interesting idea. But if the history of the world was to be affected by the successful firing of one torpedo, the plotters were expecting a lot. In that era of notoriously inefficient torpedoes, there was every reason to expect Schwieger's missile to misfire or go astray. Even in the event of a direct hit, chances are that the huge ship would have managed to limp to the nearest port a few short miles away. The odds on the ship going straight to the bottom after being hit by a single torpedo were infinitesimal. Only an extraordinary combination of circumstances made it happen the way it did.

Beyond that, the conspiracy theory overlooks an important question. Did Britain want the U.S. to enter

(Overleaf) Jason *and* Delta *investigate the great tear in the* Lusitania's *side, while* Homer *moves into the ship.*

the war at that time? Britain was already purchasing massive quantities of munitions from the United States. If the U.S. entered the war, those guns and ammunition would be needed to build up America's standing army, a process that the State Department estimated would take a year or two. A U.S. declaration of war would, initially at least, result only in the diversion of supplies that the British desperately needed. Spring Rice, the British ambassador in Washington, stated that Britain's "main interest" at this time was to keep America as a source of much-needed supplies.

Perhaps most damaging to the theory that the British had arranged the whole thing was the reaction of the Admiralty chiefs after the *Lusitania* sank. Captain Richard Webb, director of the Admiralty's trade division, was of the opinion that Cunard's New York office had been infiltrated by agents who had succeeded in finding out details of Turner's route to Liverpool. Furthermore, Webb declared that Captain Turner was guilty of "almost inconceivable negligence." First Sea Lord Jacky Fisher endorsed the sentiment with a scribbled "fully concur" in the margin of Webb's report. Webb came to the conclusion that Turner was either totally incompetent or that he had been "got at by the Germans." Fisher, barely able to control his fury, wrote, "As the Cunard Company would not have employed an *incompetent* man, the certainty is absolute that Captain Turner is not a fool but a knave!" He added his hope that Turner would be arrested "*immediately* after the [Mersey] inquiry *whatever* the verdict or finding may be. No seaman in his senses could have acted as he did," Fisher declared; he called Turner a "scoundrel."

The reactions of Churchill and Fisher present a cogent argument against the conspiracy theory. There

First Sea Lord Jacky Fisher called Captain Turner a "scoundrel" and hoped that he would be arrested.

can be little doubt that these men were outraged and embarrassed by Turner's conduct. But they couldn't say so publicly. The war still raged. To catalogue Turner's breaches was to detail the Admiralty's antisubmarine procedures and to reveal the Royal Navy's critical shortage of escort vessels.

Assuming that the conspiracy theory can be laid to rest, there have traditionally been two other explanations: one is that the "contraband" the *Lusitania* was carrying (but that no one ever saw) was set off by the torpedo; the other is that a boiler exploded.

One thing we are sure of: if any contraband had been stowed away in the magazine, it didn't explode. We were able to inspect the entire exposed area of the magazine and it was clearly undamaged. If it held munitions, they were not the cause of the secondary explosions that sank the ship. The distance between the torpedo's impact and the magazine was too great.

So if illegal cargo didn't cause the fatal explosion, what did? We rejected the boilers as the cause. None of the survivors from the three operating boiler rooms reported such an explosion.

It took us a while to realize that the clues lay all around us: chunks of coal that had fallen out of the liner as she sank. On the Atlantic run the *Lusitania* gobbled up coal at the rate of a thousand tons a day. She carried her fuel in huge bunkers located along the inside of the hull below the water line. Any torpedo would have struck the *Lusitania* bunkers. No wonder coal spilled out in these as the great ship went down.

With the aid of Cyril Spurr, a British explosives expert and former naval officer, we set out to recreate the scene at the moment of the torpedoing. The story began to take form.

After the voyage from New York, the *Lusitania*'s

hen the Lusitania *was torpedoed off Ireland (right) her coal bunkers were almost empty. The explosion (middle right) kicked up large amounts of coal dust that blanketed the bottom of the bunkers, and that the torpedo ignited (lower right), tearing open the side of the ship for the length of one of the starboard*

bunkers. The ship's magazine, (red area) remained undamaged. (Above) Coal scattered over the bottom of the sea was one of the clues that led us to believe that the second explosion was caused by ignited coal dust.

coal supply is getting low. By now she carries more coal dust than coal. Layers of the stuff form thick carpets in the bunkers on either side of the boiler rooms. The *Lusitania* burned bituminous coal, a highly combustible type. In itself the dust from this coal poses little danger, but a final ingredient is about to be added.

A torpedo slams into the ship's side and explodes. The detonation shakes the entire ship, but no part more severely than the area of the coal bunkers on the starboard side. It is as if an earthquake has struck. Violently shaken out of repose, the coal dust rises, an ominously dark cloud of it, billowing like silt disturbed from the

seabed. It has been transformed. No longer is it merely the dirty by-product of the ship's boiler rooms; it has become a highly volatile mixture force-fed with oxygen.

At the same instant, a spark or flame ignites the mixture. The result: a massive, uncontrollable explosion, a tidal wave of fire that rips through the ship's lower deck and blasts its way through the side of the hull. Within moments, the ship begins to list to starboard, as uncounted thousands of gallons of seawater pour in — a surging, smashing assault that nothing can stem.

The *Lusitania* has only minutes to live.

The *Lusitania*'s Lucky Sister

They came into the world three months apart: the *Lusitania* in June 1906, the *Mauretania* in September. For a few golden years prior to World War I, the sister ships dominated the North Atlantic.

To the casual observer the two sisters looked identical; in fact, they differed by about five feet in length (the *Mauretania* was longer), in their vents (*Lusitania*'s looked like oil drums) and in decor, layout and technical niceties. Although "Lucy-lovers" loyally claimed superiority for their favorite, the *Mauretania* had a definite edge on her older sister. In December 1910 she made world news by sailing from Britain to New York and back again in twelve days, taking a mere forty-eight hours for the "turnaround" that normally required five days and battling severe snowstorms and violent seas on her return voyage.

When the ill-fated *Lusitania* sank in May 1915, her sister was about to go into war

(Left) Mauretania *alongside the tiny* Turbinia, *the world's first turbine-powered ship.* (Right) For part of the war, the Mauretania *served as a troop ship*

and was painted in dazzle camouflage (above) *to confuse enemy ships.* (Right) The Mauretania, *in 1935 at the end of her long life, waits for the final trip to the scrapyard.*

service, carrying troops to the Dardanelles. Later she served as a hospital ship. During one wartime voyage in the Mediterranean, her skipper, Captain Dow (who had earlier commanded the *Lusitania*), spotted a torpedo in the nick of time, and as hundreds of troops and sailors watched open-mouthed, he spun her like a yacht, evading the missile with about five feet to spare.

In 1920, Cunard considered refitting the *Mauretania* for a postwar career. She was beginning to show her age. Some directors even recommended scrapping her and building an ultramodern liner. Ironically, an accident gave the *Mauretania* a new lease on life when a fire on board destroyed many cabins. During repairs, Cunard decided to convert the ship to oil power from coal. It cost £250,000, but it did wonders for the venerable liner's performance. Rejuvenated, she went on to travel the North Atlantic for another fifteen profitable years.

Epilogue

OF THE 1,959 MEN, WOMEN AND CHILDREN aboard the *Lusitania* when she pulled out of New York on May 1, 1915, 1,195 were lost: 178 saloon passengers, 374 second-cabin passengers, 239 third-class passengers and 404 crew members.

The survivors totaled 764: 113 saloon passengers,

227 second-cabin passengers, 134 third-class passengers and 290 crew members.

Statistically speaking, crew members stood a better chance of surviving the sinking than passengers; 41 percent of the crew were saved. Undeniably some looked after themselves before they worried about any passengers. Generally speaking, though, their performance was about as good as could be expected of such a crew at such a time. Many acted with commendable courage and concern for their passengers. Their familiarity with the sea, although it might not have satisfied Captain Turner, undoubtedly improved their own chances of survival;

(Previous page) Queenstown (now Cobh) as it looks today. (Above) Deaths in the Lusitania *sinking totaled 1,195 people. Unlike the* Titanic, *the* Lusitania's *losses were spread fairly evenly among the different classes aboard.*

moreover, most were young and in robust health. In general, male passengers had a slightly better survival rate than females: 38.8 percent vs 38.6 percent.

Sadly, only 27.1 percent of the children on board came through the ordeal alive.

∽

MARGARET MACKWORTH DIVORCED Sir Humphrey in 1922. She never remarried. She took over most of her father's business interests after his death in 1919; later she became editor of *Time and Tide.* She died in 1958.

A day or two after the sinking, Edith Williams and her seven-year-old brother, Edward, the only survivors of their family, found themselves in temporary accommodation at the splendid Leahy estate in Cork. They remained there for two weeks until an uncle came from England and took them back to his home. A few months later their father turned up. Edith ran away. She eventually returned to the United States. For years she was haunted by memories of the sinking; she said she felt her lost sister's tiny hand in hers for nearly twenty years.

Nurse Alice Lines and her tiny charge Audrey both survived the sinking, as did Audrey's brother. Alice and Audrey became lifelong friends. Avis Dolphin and Ian Holbourn also survived the sinking. They too remained friends. Holbourn wrote about the sinking

Today this memorial commemorating the sinking stands in the central square in Cobh.

STOC ARN I NRA NIM ÖÉ

TO THE MEMORY OF ALL WHO PERISHED BY
SINKING OF THE LUSITANIA MAY·7·1915
AND IN THE CAUSE OF UNIVERSAL AND
LASTING ...

·LABORARE EST ORARE·
HELPED IN THE RESCUE·GAVE AID AND COMFORT
TO THE SURVIVORS AND BURIED THE DEAD

D. CORCORAN

A vis Dolphin Foley (above) as she looks today, still going strong. She remained lifelong friends with Ian Holbourn, the man whose quick actions saved her life. (Above right) Nurse Alice Lines, left, and her former charge Audrey Pearl are still close friends. (Below left) Alfred Bestic was torpedoed again during World War II and once more managed to survive. Bestic was one of the last visitors Captain Turner (below right) had before his death in 1933. (Below middle) Edith and Edward were the only two surviving members of the Williams family.

in his 1936 book, *The Isle of Foula*. Avis lives in Wales.

On September 7, 1915, four months to the day after the sinking of the *Lusitania*, a leather case was delivered to Mrs. Julia Sullivan at Clounlea, Kilgarvan, County Kerry. It was part of her baggage that had been lost during the sinking. Eventually, the case had washed ashore. Not a penny of the cash and gold it contained was missing.

Eighteen months after the sinking, the *U-20* ran aground in thick fog off the Danish coast. Although every effort was made to refloat her, the task proved impossible. She was blown up by the detonation of two torpedoes in her tubes.

Walther Schwieger went on to command the *U-88*, a larger and more powerful vessel than the *U-20*. Although it was widely reported that he received a special medal for sinking the *Lusitania*, this was not true. In July 1917 he was awarded the *Pour le Mérite* for the 190,000 tons of Allied shipping he had destroyed. The *Lusitania* was not mentioned in the citation. Two months later Schwieger and his crew disappeared at sea, apparently having run into a mine.

R ecently, the Daily Express *reported that a group of divers who visited the* Lusitania *in the summer of 1994 had noticed circular lead containers on the bottom. These containers, they allege, hold paintings by Rubens, Titian and others that Sir Hugh Lane (top) was accompanying from New York for eventual delivery to Dublin's National Gallery. Famed Edwardian art dealer Lord Duveen (bottom) had set up the deal. Lane did not survive the sinking and the paintings went down with the ship. Some say the paintings would have perished long ago, but the Irish government is looking into the story, and has placed a preservation order on the wreck to protect it and any surviving cargo.*

❦

TWO MEN WERE THE ARCHITECTS OF THE *LUSITANIA* tragedy: Walther Schwieger and William Turner. We shall never know whether Schwieger knew his target to be the *Lusitania*, or whether he thought her to be her sister ship, the *Mauretania*, which at that time was being fitted out for use as a troop transport and as such was a perfectly legitimate target. In his log Schwieger claimed that he was unaware of his victim's identity until he spotted the name on the ship's bow as she went down.

William Turner was probably guilty of ignorance and lack of flexibility more than anything else. A simple man who had spent his working life aboard ship, Turner grew up in a time of unchanging values. In his world, naval vessels did not sink ships full of civilians, with or without warning. It's doubtful whether he ever gave much thought to the acres of directives that the Admiralty kept sending his way.

He set off from New York on May 1, 1915, in an innocent age.

When he landed at Queenstown, Ireland, a bedraggled survivor of the sinking, a harsher, crueler era had already begun. His tragedy was that he didn't know it.

A LUSITANIA CHRONOLOGY

*Compiled by
Eric and Bill Sauder.*

CHRONOLOGY
1902
First preliminary designs
submitted for the
Lusitania and the *Mauretania*,
depicting them with only
three funnels.

(Above) The Lusitania's
*keel takes shape. (Previous page)
The* Lusitania *steaming off the Old
Head of Kinsale in peacetime.*

JUNE 16, 1904
Lusitania's first keel plate laid.

JUNE 6, 1906
Lusitania is launched by
Mary, Lady Inverclyde, before
a crowd of thousands.

JULY 27, 1907
Lusitania undergoes
preliminary trials off Ireland with
a number of guests on board.

JULY–AUGUST 1907
Lusitania goes through formal
acceptance trials.

H er hull nearly ready for launching, the Lusitania *towers over the John Brown yards in Scotland's Clydebank.*

(Top) *A baggage tag
and* (above) *a souvenir postcard.*

SEPTEMBER 3, 1907
Lusitania is opened to the public
and 20,000 people visit her.

SEPTEMBER 7, 1907
Lusitania leaves Liverpool on
her maiden voyage.

SEPTEMBER 13, 1907
Lusitania arrives in New York
for the first time.

OCTOBER 1907
Lusitania wins back the
Blue Riband for Great Britain
from Germany.

OCTOBER–NOVEMBER, 1907
Mauretania undergoes her
official trials.

NOVEMBER 16, 1907
Mauretania departs for New York
on her maiden voyage.

DECEMBER 1910
Mauretania sets a speed
record for a two-way crossing,
from Liverpool to New York and
back again in twelve days,
including a scant two-day
stopover in New York. This
record was set despite severe
storms on the homeward leg
of the journey.

JULY 11, 1913
Captain William Turner
receives King George V and
Queen Mary aboard *Mauretania*
and gives them a guided
tour of the liner.

AUGUST 4, 1914
Britain declares war on
Germany. *Mauretania* is at sea
at the time and makes a

28-knot dash to the safety
of New York.

NOVEMBER 1914
The number of crossings for
Lusitania is reduced to one per
month. The ship's number four
boiler room is shut down to save
on coal, reducing her maximum
speed to 21 knots.

FEBRUARY 1915
Germans declare waters around
Great Britain a war zone in which
ships may be sunk without
warning. *Lusitania* flies American
flag as protection against
German submarines.

MAY 1, 1915
Lusitania leaves New York
for the last time.

The Mauretania *and the* Lusitania *pass in Liverpool's River Mersey.*

The Lusitania *goes down off Ireland, May 7, 1915.*

MAY 7, 1915
Lusitania torpedoed and sunk with 1,195 fatalities. Later that same year, the first salvage proposals are made; all are impracticable.

1915-1918
During World War One, *Mauretania* serves as a troop transport and hospital ship.

1919
After the war, Germany is forced to surrender her premier liner, *Imperator*, to replace *Lusitania*. Cunard renames her *Berengaria*.

JUNE 1921
Mauretania catches fire at pierside in Southampton and suffers considerable damage. During repairs, Cunard takes the opportunity to convert her coal-burning boilers to oil, increasing her speed.

1929
Mauretania loses Blue Riband to Germany's new superliner, *Bremen*.

EARLY 1930s
Transatlantic business is severely affected by the Great Depression. Cunard reassigns *Mauretania* to cruising, a then-lucrative business thanks in part to U.S. Prohibition, which drives Americans onto foreign-owned ships where alcohol is served.

SEPTEMBER 1934
Cunard's merger with former archrival White Star results in considerable surplus tonnage. *Mauretania* is retired and her fittings auctioned off.

1935
The *Lusitania* wreck is located with early echo-sounding equipment.

1935
The salvage vessel *Ophir* anchors above the wreck, and a memorial service is held for the *Lusitania*.

Diver Jim Jarrat, clad in a bulky diving suit, visits the wreck, the first person to see the ship since she sank twenty years before.

Mauretania is scrapped.

For the next two decades, gossip on the Irish coast reports that the British Admiralty is conducting blasting operations on the wreck of the *Lusitania*.

The "top of the house" aboard the Mauretania.

1953
Divers state that the wreck is lying on her starboard side, not port as Jarrat had previously reported.

EARLY 1960s
John Light starts diving operations on *Lusitania*.

JANUARY 1968
Gregg Bemis and partners buy
the salvage rights from Light.

SEPTEMBER-OCTOBER 1982
Oceaneering International mounts
an expedition to the wreck and
recovers a number of artifacts.
Ireland attempts to claim recovered
items as national treasures. Courts
rule in favor of the salvagers.

(Above) The Mauretania in harbor.
(Left) Robert Ballard and team aboard
the Northern Horizon, 1993.

1983
Oceaneering International plans
to return to the wreck this year
to document cargo hold, but the
expedition never takes place.

1989
Salvaged whistle and bell sold at
auction by Sotheby's of London.

JULY–AUGUST 1993
Ballard expedition visits the
wreck of the Lusitania.

*"Although time fades and
the little gray cells get worn out, I can
still sit here now and see the liner...
just sliding beneath the waves."*

Eyewitness George Henderson recalling the
sinking of the *Lusitania* eighty years ago.

———❖———

(Below) The last picture of the Lusitania,
on her final voyage.

End Matter

Acknowledgments

M ANY, MANY PEOPLE AIDED IN MAKING OUR 1993 expedition to the *Lusitania* such a success. Although I could never thank everyone who contributed, there are a number of people who deserve special mention.

First off, I would like to thank all the people from the Woods Hole Oceanographic Institution. Woods Hole was my first "exploring" home, and I am grateful for the continued help I have received from Andy Bowen, Dave Mindell, Bob Elder, Will Sellars, Dana Yoerger, Jon Howland and Linda Lucier. Thanks also to my two long-time friends from the Marquest Group, Cathy Offinger and Martin Bowen.

Thanks are due to everyone connected to our mini-submarine *Delta* — Richard Slater, Chris Ijames, Kent Barnard and David Slater, to Andy Clark and Jerry Neely at Harbor Branch Oceanographic Institution, and to Simon Allen at Seaway and Captain Neal Emory and the crew of the *Northern Horizon*.

Throughout this expedition, as on our earlier quests, the National Geographic Society provided us with tremendous assistance. At National Geographic Television, I would like to thank Tim Kelly, Susan Borke, Peter Schnall, Bruce Norfleet, Scott Breindel and Rick Gioia. At National Geographic magazine, thanks must be given to Peter Miller, Keith Moorehead, Larry Nighswander and Jonathan Blair, National Geographic's photographer.

Further thanks for their visual efforts must be given to Paul Matthias of Polaris Consulting, who created the computer maps of the *Lusitania* from our sonar scans, and to Mark Shelley and Jeff Hogan, of Sea Studio, who were responsible for the underwater video work.

In Ireland, I want to thank the people at the Cobh Heritage Museum for the help they gave us, the people at Celtic Diving and Salvage, specifically Mike Whelan and the captain and crew of the tug *Alert*. A very special thanks to Bill O'Mahony and Finbarr Golden of Southern Port Sevices/Cork Bonded Warehouse and Mr. Paddy O'Sullivan.

Finally, I would like to thank F. Gregg Bemis, for granting us permission to dive on the wreck, Ken Marschall for his inspiring paintings, our two historians, Bill Sauder and Eric Sauder, Cyril Spurr for helping us to solve the mystery of the *Lusitania,* David Weil for his continued support and guidance, the Titanic Historical Society and last, but by no means least, my wife, Barbara, for assistance and inspiration beyond words.

MADISON PRESS BOOKS AND SPENCER DUNMORE WOULD like to thank the staff at the Canadian War Museum Library in Ottawa, Ontario, and at the Mills Memorial Library of McMaster University in Hamilton, Ontario; the Colindale Newspaper Library in London, England; Eric Sauder for carefully vetting the manuscript and for his research for Ken Marschall's paintings, and his brothers Chris and Bill, who contributed extensive unpaid expertise; Mark Reynolds of Burlington,

Ontario, for technical advice and for the loan of numerous *Lusitania*-related items from his personal collection; thanks also to Dori Chappell and Betty Behnke at National Geographic for providing the underwater pictures reproduced in this book and to Bruce Norfleet at National Geographic Television for the transcripts of interviews with survivors.

FINALLY, THANKS TO CHRISSIE AITKEN BARNETT, DESMOND Cox, Alice Lines Drury, Avis Dolphin Foley, Elsie Hook Hadland, Frank Hook, Audrey Pearl Lawson Johnston, Cecil Richards, Edith Williams Wachtel, John Edward Williams and Nancy Wickings-Smith Woods, all survivors of the *Lusitania* disaster, whose reminiscences about that terrible day were indispensable in putting this book together.

Photograph and Illustration Credits

Every effort has been made to attribute all material reproduced in this book correctly. If any errors have occurred, we shall be happy to correct them in future editions.

Front jacket painting by Ken Marschall.

1 Collection of Eric Sauder.

2–3 Jonathan Blair © National Geographic Society.

4–5 Brown Brothers.

6–7 National Maritime Museum (Greenwich), D4726/11. Photograph from collection of Eric Sauder.

8–9 Painting by Ken Marschall.

CHAPTER ONE

10–11 Robert D. Ballard © Odyssey Corporation.

12–13 Stanford University.

14 Mary Evans Picture Library.

16–17 Robert D. Ballard © Odyssey Corporation.

16 (bottom) Jonathan Blair © National Geographic Society.

17 (bottom left) Robert D. Ballard © Odyssey Corporation.

17 (bottom right) Robert D. Ballard © Odyssey Corporation.

18 (top) Collection of Eric Sauder.

18 (middle) Collection of Eric Sauder.

19 Brown Brothers.

20 (top left) University of Glasgow. Photograph from collection of Eric Sauder.

20 (bottom left) Scottish Record Office, 144/9. Photograph from collection of Eric Sauder.

20 (right) Collection of Eric Sauder.

21 Brown Brothers.

22–23 Collection of Eric Sauder.

CHAPTER TWO

24–25 Collection of Eric Sauder.

26 (top) Brown Brothers.

26 (middle) Brown Brothers.

26 (bottom left) Collection of Eric Sauder.

26 (bottom right) Collection of Eric Sauder.

27 Bettmann Archive, U-18138-INP.

28 (top) Collection of Eric Sauder.

28 (bottom) Bettmann Archive, U-30097-INP.

29 (top) Museum of the City of New York, Byron Collection, 1481/24809. Photograph from collection of Eric Sauder.

29 (bottom) Brown Brothers.

31 Bettmann Archive, 26-WB.

32 Brown Brothers.

33 (top) Scottish Record Office. Photograph from collection of Eric Sauder.

33 (bottom left) Collection of Eric Sauder.

33 (bottom right) Bettmann Archive, U-18816-NY.

34 National Maritime Museum (Greenwich), D4726/8. Photograph from collection of Eric Sauder.

35 (top) Collection of Eric Sauder.

35 (middle) Collection of Eric Sauder.

35 (bottom left) Collection of Eric Sauder.

35 (bottom right) Collection of Eric Sauder.

36 (left) Scottish Record Office, 136/10. Photograph from collection of Eric Sauder.

36 (right) Collection of Eric Sauder.

37 Brown Brothers.

38 (left) Bibliothek für Zeitgeschichte, Stuttgart, 240/12.

38 (right) Bibliothek für Zeitgeschichte, Stuttgart, 240/5.

39 (top) Map by Jack McMaster.

39 (bottom) The Mariners'
Museum, Newport News,
Virginia, A-PB-97/V.62.
Photograph from
collection of Eric Sauder.

∂∞

CHAPTER THREE

40–41 Collection of Eric Sauder.
42–43 Painting by
Ken Marschall.
44 (top) Brown Brothers.
44 (middle) Brown Brothers.
44 (bottom) Bettmann Archive,
VV-1357.
46 (top) Brown Brothers.
46 (bottom) Collection of
Ken Marschall.
47 Collection of Mark Warren.
48–49 Collection of Eric Sauder.
48 (inset) Collection of Eric
Sauder.
50–51 (top) Collection of
Eric Sauder.
50 (bottom) Collection of
Eric Sauder.
51 (top) Collection of Ken
Marschall.
51 (middle) Collection of
Eric Sauder.
51 (bottom left) Collection of
Eric Sauder.
51 (bottom right) Collection of
Eric Sauder.
52–53 Museum of the City of
New York, Byron Collection,
1481/24794. Photograph
from collection of
Eric Sauder.
53 (top) Collection of Eric Sauder.
53 (bottom) Collection of
Eric Sauder.
54 (top) Scottish Record Office.
Photograph from collection of
Eric Sauder
54 (left) Collection of Eric Sauder.
54 (right) Collection of
Eric Sauder.

55 (top right) Collection of
Eric Sauder.
55 (top left) Collection of
Mark Reynolds.
55 (middle) Collection of
Eric Sauder.
55 (bottom) Byron Collection,
Museum of the City
of New York, 93.1.1.11304.
56 (top) Scottish Record Office.
Photograph from
collection of Eric Sauder.
56 (bottom left) Collection of
Eric Sauder.
56 (bottom right) Collection of
Eric Sauder.
57 (far top) Collection of
Eric Sauder.
57 (middle top) Collection of
Eric Sauder.
57 (middle bottom) Collection of
Eric Sauder.
57 (bottom) Collection of
Eric Sauder.
58 Scottish Record Office,
145/13. Photograph from
collection of Eric Sauder.
58 (inset) Collection of Eric
Sauder.
60 Collection of Eric Sauder.
61 (left) Collection of Eric Sauder.
61 (right) Collection of
Eric Sauder.
62 Collection of Frank Braynard.
62 (inset) Bettmann Archive,
VV-1474.
63 Collection of Eric Sauder.
64–65 Bibliothek für
Zeitgeschichte,
Stuttgart, 240/4.
65 Map by Jack McMaster.
66–67 Painting by Claus Bergen.
Erich Lessing/Art Resource,
New York, 27-01-01/16.
68 (top left) Bibliothek für
Zeitgeschichte,
Stuttgart, 240/7.

68 (top right) Brown Brothers.
68 (bottom) Popperfoto.
69 Imperial War Museum,
London, Q-18124.
70 (top left) Bibliothek für
Zeitgeschichte, Stuttgart,
137/23.
70 (middle) Bibliothek für
Zeitgeschichte, Stuttgart,
240/10.
70 Bibliothek für Zeitgeschichte,
Stuttgart, 240/11.
71 Ullstein Bilderdienst,
6 60097-5.

∂∞

CHAPTER FOUR

72–73 Collection of Eric Sauder.
75 Painting by Achille Beltrame,
from *Domenica del Corriere*,
Rizzoli Periodici, Milan.
76–77 Bettmann Archive, 213.27.
79 Hulton Deutsch Collection,
02811138.
80 Bettmann Archive,
UPI-733218-INP.
82 (top) Collection of Eric Sauder.
82 (bottom) Map by
Jack McMaster.
83 Süddeutscher Verlag
Bilderdienst.
84–85 (top) Painting by Felix
Schwormstadt, courtesy
Bildarchiv Preussischer
Kulturbesitz, F-2075-b.
84 (left inset) Ullstein
Bilderdienst, 6 60131-2.
84–85 (bottom) Diagram by
Jack McMaster.

∂∞

CHAPTER FIVE

86 *The Sphere*. Photograph
collection of Eric Sauder.
88–89 Painting by
Ken Marschall.
91 (left) Mary Evans Picture
Library.
91 (right) Collection of
Eric Sauder.

92–93 Diagram by Jack McMaster.

94–95 *The Sphere*. Collection of Eric Sauder.

96–97 Painting by Ken Marschall.

100 Bettmann Archive, U-27757-INP.

101 Collection of Eric Sauder.

103 Collection of Eric Sauder.

106–107 Painting by Ken Marschall.

108 *The Illustrated London News*. Photograph from collection of Eric Sauder.

109 Mary Evans Picture Library.

110 Diagram by Jack McMaster.

111 (top) Collection of Eric Sauder.

111 (inset) Collection of Eric Sauder.

112 Mary Evans Picture Library.

113 Bettmann Archive, U-27755-INP.

114 (top) Mansell Collection.

114 (bottom left) Hulton Deutsch Collection, 02811626.

114 (bottom right) Collection of Eric Sauder.

115 (top) Hulton Deutsch Collection, 04017433.

115 (bottom) Bettmann Archive, U-27751-INP.

116 (top) Brown Brothers.

116 (bottom) Bettmann Archive, U-27192-INP.

117 Brown Brothers.

CHAPTER SIX

118 Hulton Deutsch Collection, 04017430.

119 Mary Evans Picture Library.

120 John Frost Historical Newspaper Collection.

121 (top left) John Frost Historical Newspaper Collection.

121 (top right) John Frost Historical Newspaper Collection.

121 (middle) John Frost Historical Newspaper Collection.

122 *Cork Examiner*. Photograph collection of Eric Sauder.

123 Bettmann Archive, U-27753-INP.

124 (left) Bettmann Archive, PL-5701.

124 (right) Bettmann Archive, 3406-RAU.

125 The Mariners' Museum, PB-17923.

126 Hulton Deutsch Collection, 04017428.

127 (left) Courtesy of the Library of Congress, POS-C-Ger-A01-48.

127 (right) Bettmann Archive, CU-368.

128–129 Bettmann Archive, U-27745-INP.

128 (bottom) Collection of Eric Sauder.

129 (bottom) Bettmann/Hulton, HPL-8368.

130 (top) Bettmann Archive, PL-6065.

130 (middle) Hulton Deutsch Collection, 01848178.

130 (bottom) Hulton Deutsch Collection, 01848224.

131 Hulton Deutsch Collection, 04017434.

133 Bettmann Archive, VV-1475.

134 Brown Brothers.

135 (left) © Alan Crisp/Retrograph Archive Ltd., London.

135 (right) © Alan Crisp/Retrograph Archive Ltd., London.

137 Bettmann Archive, U-143475-INP.

138 (top) Bettmann Archive, PL-7695.

138 (middle) Bettmann Archive, SF-7699.

138 (bottom) Collection of Mark Reynolds.

139 Mary Evans Picture Library.

140 Masterfile FPH-01-00141.

141 Collection of Eric Sauder.

142 Stanford University.

143 (top) Stanford University.

143 (middle) Stanford University.

143 (bottom) Bettmann Archive, SF-7700.

CHAPTER SEVEN

144 Jonathan Blair © National Geographic Society.

145 Painting by Ken Marschall.

146 (top) Robert D. Ballard © Odyssey Corporation.

146 (middle) Robert D. Ballard © Odyssey Corporation.

146 (bottom) Courtesy of Odyssey Corporation.

147 Robert D. Ballard © Odyssey Corporation.

148 Courtesy of Odyssey Corporation.

149 (top) Polaris Consulting. Picture courtesy of Odyssey Corporation.

149 (bottom) Polaris Consulting. Picture courtesy of Odyssey Corporation.

150 Robert D. Ballard © Odyssey Corporation.

151 (top) Robert D. Ballard © Odyssey Corporation.

151 (middle) Robert D. Ballard © Odyssey Corporation.

151 (bottom) Robert D. Ballard © Odyssey Corporation.

153 Jonathan Blair © National Geographic Society.

CHAPTER EIGHT

154–155 Jonathan Blair ©
National Geographic Society.

155 (top) Picture courtesy of
Odyssey Corporation.

155 (bottom) Collection of
Eric Sauder.

156 (top) Jonathan Blair ©
National Geographic Society.

156 (bottom) Jonathan Blair ©
National Geographic Society.

157 Jonathan Blair © National
Geographic Society.
Photograph from collection of
Eric Sauder.

157 (inset) Collection of
Eric Sauder.

158–159 Painting by
Ken Marschall.

160–162 Painting by
Ken Marschall.

163–165 Diagram by
Jack McMaster.

166 Jonathan Blair © National
Geographic Society.

166 (left) Jonathan Blair ©
National Geographic Society.

166 (right) Collection of
Eric Sauder.

167 (top) Jonathan Blair ©
National Geographic Society.

167 (bottom) Jonathan Blair ©
National Geographic Society.

168 Jonathan Blair © National
Geographic Society.

168 (inset) Collection of
Eric Sauder.

169 (left) Collection of
Eric Sauder.

169 (top right) Jonathan Blair ©
National Geographic Society.

169 (middle) Jonathan Blair ©
National Geographic Society.

169 (bottom right) Jonathan
Blair © National Geographic
Society.

170–171 Jonathan Blair ©
National Geographic Society.

171 (inset top) Collection of
Eric Sauder.

171 (inset bottom) Jonathan Blair
© National Geographic
Society.

172 Jonathan Blair © National
Geographic Society.

173 (bottom left) Collection of
Eric Sauder.

173 (middle bottom) Collection
of Eric Sauder.

173 (bottom right) Collection of
Eric Sauder.

173 (top) Jonathan Blair ©
National Geographic Society.

173 (middle) Jonathan Blair ©
National Geographic Society.

174 (top) Collection of
Eric Sauder.

174 (bottom) Jonathan Blair ©
National Geographic Society.
Photograph from collection of
Eric Sauder.

175 (top) Collection of
Eric Sauder.

175 (bottom) Jonathan Blair ©
National Geographic Society.
Photograph from collection of
Eric Sauder.

176–177 Jonathan Blair ©
National Geographic Society.

178 (inset) Collection of
Eric Sauder.

178–179 Jonathan Blair ©
National Geographic Society.

180–181 Jonathan Blair ©
National Geographic Society.
Photograph from collection of
Eric Sauder.

181 (top) Collection of
Eric Sauder.

181 (middle) Jonathan Blair ©
National Geographic Society.

181 (bottom) Collection of
Eric Sauder.

182–183 Jonathan Blair ©
National Geographic Society.

182 (inset left) Jonathan Blair ©
National Geographic Society.

183 (inset right) Collection of
Eric Sauder.

184 (top) Jonathan Blair ©
National Geographic Society.
Photograph from collection of
Eric Sauder.

184 (middle) Jonathan Blair ©
National Geographic Society.
Photograph from collection of
Eric Sauder.

184 (bottom) Scottish Record
Office. Photograph from
collection of Eric Sauder.

185 Robert D. Ballard ©
Odyssey Corporation.

186–187 Jonathan Blair ©
National Geographic Society.

187 (inset) Collection of Eric
Sauder.

188 Painting by Ken Marschall.

189 (top) Jonathan Blair ©
National Geographic Society.

189 (middle) Jonathan Blair ©
National Geographic Society.

189 (bottom) Jonathan Blair ©
National Geographic Society.

CHAPTER NINE

190 Hulton Deutsch Collection,
04027789.

191 Jonathan Blair © National
Geographic Society.

192–193 Painting by
Ken Marschall.

194 Mary Evans Picture Library.

195 (left) Jonathan Blair ©
National Geographic Society.

195 (right) Illustration by
Jack McMaster.

196 The Science Museum/Science
and Society Picture Library,
South Kensington, No. 7043.

197 (top) Brown Brothers.
197 (middle) Imperial War
Museum, London.
197 (bottom) Collection of
Eric Sauder.

❧

CHAPTER TEN
198–199 Robert D. Ballard ©
Odyssey Corporation.
200 Diagram by Jack McMaster.
201 Collection of Eric Sauder.
202 (top left) Jonathan Blair ©
National Geographic Society.
202 (top right) Jonathan Blair ©
National Geographic Society.
202 (center) Collection of
Eric Sauder.
202 (bottom left) Collection of
Eric Sauder.

202 (bottom right) Collection of
Eric Sauder.
203 (top) Mansell Collection.
203 (bottom) Hulton Deutsch
Collection, 04135729
204–205 Imperial War Museum,
London, Q-48349.
204–205 Painting by Ken
Marschall.
206 (left) Collection of
Eric Sauder.
206–207 Collection of
Eric Sauder.
208 (top) Collection of
Eric Sauder.
208 (middle) Collection of
Eric Sauder.
208 (bottom) National Maritime
Museum (Greenwich),
61/316.

209 (top) Mary Evans Picture
Library.
209 (bottom) Brown Brothers.
210–211 Jonathan Blair ©
National Geographic Society.
211 The Mariner's Museum,
PB-13522.

❧

BACK JACKET
Photograph from collection
of Eric Sauder.
(Inset left) Jonathan Blair ©
National Geographic Society.
(Inset center) Jonathan Blair ©
National Geographic Society.
(Inset right) Jonathan Blair ©
National Geographic Society.

Bibliography

Bailey, T.A., and P.B. Ryan. *The Lusitania Disaster*. New York: Free Press, 1975.

Botting, Douglas. *The U-Boats*. The Seafarers Series. Amsterdam: Time-Life Books, 1979.

Dear, Ian. *Great Ocean Liners: The Heyday of Luxury Travel*. London: B.T. Batsford, 1977.

Hall, Cyril. *Modern Weapons of War*. London: Blackie and Son, 1915.

Hickey, Des, and Gus Smith. *Seven Days to Disaster*. New York: G.P. Putnam's Sons, 1981.

Hoehling, A.A., and Mary Hoehling. *The Last Voyage of the Lusitania*. London: Longmans, Green and Co., 1975.

Maxtone-Graham, John. *The Only Way to Cross*. New York: Macmillan Publishing, 1972.

Miller, William H., Jr. *The First Great Ocean Liners in Photographs: 193 Views, 1897-1927*. New York: Dover Publications, 1984.

Ransome-Wallis, P. *North Atlantic Panorama, 1900-1976*. London: Ian Allan, 1977.

Rhondda, Viscountess (Margaret Mackworth). *This Was My World*. London: Macmillan, 1933.

Sauder, Eric, with Ken Marschall. *R.M.S. Lusitania: Triumph of the Edwardian Age*. Redondo Beach: Trans-Atlantic Designs, 1991.

Simpson, Colin. *The Lusitania*. London: Longmans, 1972.

Wall, Robert. *Ocean Liners*. London: Collins, 1978.

Warren, Mark D., ed. *Lusitania: The Cunard Turbine-driven Quadruple-screw Atlantic Liner*. Wellingborough: Patrick Stevens Ltd, 1986.

Index

A

Aboukir, sunk by *U-9*, 70

Aitken, Chrissie, 27–28, 59, 78; at moment of torpedo impact, 87, 90–91; during sinking, 104; identifies dead father, 116; survives, 116, 117

Aitken, James, death of, 116

Aitken, Jarvie, 28, 59

Aitken, Jarvie Junior, 59, 78, 90

Ambulances, named after *Lusitania*, *135*

Anderson, Staff Captain John, 59, 101

Aquitania, 100

Aspinall, Butler, 132, 136

B

Balfour, Arthur, 18

Ballard, Barbara, 10, 16

Ballard, Robert, *16*; views on access to historic wrecks, 147–148

Bandon (Ireland), 10, 100

Bemis, Gregg, 147

Bergensfjord, 30

Bernard, Oliver, 35, 72; at moment of torpedo impact, 87, 90; describes victims, 115; doubts about lifeboats of, 63; during sinking, 102, 105, 108; survives, 117

Bestic, Third Officer Albert, *100*, 100–101, *202*; survival of, 108–110

Birkenhead, Earl of, *see* Smith, Sir Frederick

Bismarck, 16, 144

Blockades, naval, 16, 68, 69, 143; rules of conduct in short-lived, 71

Blue Riband, 18, 21, 147, 155

Bluebell (rescue ship), 112, 115

Board of Trade, 63; inquiry of 132–133, *133*

Booth, Alfred, 135

Booth, Lady, *135*

Bowen, Andy, 16

Bowen, Martin, 16, 146, *148*

Britannic, 100

British Expeditionary Force, 78

Brow Head (Ireland), 79

Bryan, William Jennings, *124*, 126

C

Cameronia, commandeered as troop ship, 28, 29

Canada, 28, 29

Candidate, sunk by *U-20*, 74

Cape Clear (Ireland), 78

Cape Matapan (Greece), 137

Carson, Sir Edward Henry, 132

Casement, Sir Roger, 132

Castle, Irene, 45

Castle, Vernon, 45

Centurion, sunk by *U-20*, 77

Churchill, Winston, 78, *190*; blamed for sinking, 14, 190,

Citizen (Ottawa), response to sinking, 123

Clydebank (Scotland), 20, 21

Coal, 30; cause of second explosion on *Lusitania*, 194–195, *195*

Cobh (Queenstown, Ireland), *see* Queenstown

Code, message sent to *Lusitania*, 79

Coke, Vice-Admiral, 78, 79, 100

Conner, Dorothy, 60, 81; during sinking, 94, 98, 105; survives, 116

Conspiracy, causes of sinking and, 14, 190, 194

Constantinople (Istanbul), 38

Courier Journal (Louisville), response to sinking, 123

Cressy, sunk by *U-9*, 70

Crew (*Lusitania*), competence of, 137, 199; dangers at sea for, 83; inexperience of, 59, 81, 137; inexperience with lifeboats, 63, 97, 134; no charges against in New York inquiry, 137; snobs among, 32

Cromptons, The, death of, 116

Cunard, 18, 22; not liable for sinking, 135–136

D

Daily Express, 203

Daily Mirror, The, reports sinking, *121*

Daily Sketch, reports sinking, *121*

Dardanelles, 38, 63, 126, 197

Debris, at sinking, 105; on wreck, 152, 189

Delta, 15, *17*, 144, *145*, 146, *150–151*, 151–152, *153*, 157, 175, 193; trapped by nets on wreck, 152, *188*, 189

Department of Commerce and Labor (U. S.), 27

Depth bomb, found on wreck, 152

Destroyers, effective against U-boats, 64

Deutschland, 18

Diving, early gear for, 14

Dolphin, Avis, 35, *35*, 46, 63, *202*, 203; at point of torpedo impact, 98–99; during sinking, 104; survival of, 200

Dow, Captain, saves *Mauretania*, 197

Dowie (stokers' mascot), deserts ship, 27

Dreadnought, 67, *68*

Drummond, Captain John (*Aboukir* commander), 70

Duveen, Lord, 203

E

Earl of Lathom, sunk by *U-20*, 74

Edinburgh, 117

Edward VII (King of England), 152

Ellis, Hilda, 98, 99, 104

Emden (Germany), 37, 38

Empress of Ireland, 113

Evasive action, 190; *see also* Zigzagging

Explosives, on board *Lusitania*, rumors of, 14

F

First Class (Saloon), amenities of, 46; barber shop, *51*; dining room, 45, *48–49*; lounge, 45, *50–51*; number of passengers, 37; reading and writing room, *51*; smoking room, *51*; verandah café, *53*

Fisher, Howard, 60, 81; during sinking, 94, 98, 105; survives, 116

Fisher, First Sea Lord Jacky, 194, *194*

Fishing nets, snagged on wreck 148, 149, 152, 167, 174, 189

Flags, flying of other countries' by combatants, 64, 71, 126

Flamm, Oswald, 190

Ford, Henry, 152

French, Sir John, 78

Frohman, Charles, *32*, 59; character of, 32, 35; death of, 116; warned against travel on *Lusitania*, 32, 37

Funnels, significance of number of, 81

G

Galley Head (Ireland), 79
Gallipoli (Turkey), battle of, 38
Gas, poison, 126
George V (King of England), in
    propaganda, 141
Gerard, James W., 190
German Embassy, newspaper
    warning to passengers from,
    31, *31*, 60, 137
Germans, attacked by mobs after
    sinking, 118, *119*; propaganda
    against after sinking,
    140; response to sinking,
    126, 143; rumors about
    Lusitania and, 37; U. S.
    opinion of, 125, 143
Germany, opinions on sinking of
    Lusitania, 126
Gimbel Brothers, 31
Glitra, sunk by *U-17*, 71
Golders Green (London), 60
Great War, 13
Gulflight, U. S. ship damaged by
    U-boat, 124, *125*

H

Harbor Branch Oceanographic
    Institution, 146

Hardman and Peck, 31
Henderson Family, watches
    Lusitania sink, 100
Herald (New York), response to
    sinking, 123
Heron, 127
Hobson, Richmond, 190
Hogue, sunk by *U-9*, 70
Holbourn, Ian, 63, *63*, 200;
    during sinking, 99; survival
    of, 200; *The Isle of Foula*
    by, 203
Homer, 15, 144, 146, *146*,
    151, 190, *191*
Horgan, John J. (Coroner),
    127, 132
Hubbard, Elbert, 35, *116*; death
    of, 116; *Message to Garcia*,
    novel by, 35
Hudson River, 39, 40, 44

I

Ijames, Chris, 152, 189
Illustrated London News, The, 117
Illustrierte Unterhaltungs
    (Germany), reports
    sinking, *121*
Imperial Grand Fleet, 67
Inquiries, guilt ascribed during
    135, 136, 137; (England),

132–133; (Ireland), 127, 132;
    (New York), 136
International Horse Breeder's
    Association, 32
Inverclyde, Lady, 21
Inverclyde, Lord, 18; death of, 21
Irish Navy, use of *Lusitania* for
    target practice by, 152
Iron Cross, 71
Ivernia, torpedoed, 137

J

Jarrat, Jim, 14, 15, 151
Jason, 15, 16, *17*, 144, *144*, 146,
    146, 148, 149
John Brown Shipyards, 20, 21
John Bull, in propaganda, 141
Juno, outruns *U-20*, 78

K

Kaiser, the Beast of Berlin, The
    (propaganda film), 143
Kaiser Wilhelm der Grosse, 18
Kennedy Space Center, 15
Klein, Charles, *116*; death of 116;
    Potash and Perlmutter by, 116
Kolnische Volkszeitung, reports
    sinking, 126

L

Lane, Sir Hugh, 203

Lansing, Robert, 126

Lanz (*U-20* pilot), 64, 77

Leith, Robert (wireless officer), 79, *79*

Life belts, 93, 98, 102, 105, 128; from *Lusitania* found in Delaware River, 134, *134*; questions about at inquiries, 132

Lifeboats, conditions on, 108; crew competence and, 100–101, 134, 137; drill not received by passengers, 63, 93, 101, 127; launching of chaotic, 94–95, 97, 103, 104; many unlaunched, 106; inquiries and, 128, 137; preparation of, 72, 137; safety procedures and, *62*, 63; *Titanic* and, 132

Life rafts, 101

Light, John, 14, 151

Lindsay, William, 35

Lines, Nurse Alice, *101, 202*; during sinking, 101–102, 104; survival of, 200

Liverpool, 13, 37, 78, 87

Lord and Taylor, 31, 93

Lusitania: ambulances named after, 135, *135*; armaments on board, question of, 14, 135–136; boiler rooms on, 100, *178*; bridge of, *29*; bulkhead doors and, 128, 137; calmness of sea for, 82; camouflage paint on, 42; capacity of, 21; cargo of, 27, 79; class distinctions on board, 31–32 (*see also*, First Class; Second Class; Third Class); coal on, *27*, 194–195; convertability into warship of, 20; design improved over *Titanic*, 23; explosives on board, questions of, 27, 136; faster than U-boats, 64; first dinner on, 60; first launch of, *20, 21, 21*, 196; food on board, 60; fuelling of, 26–27; last voyage, ease of, 83; last voyage, photo from, *44*; length of, 20; lifeboats on adequate, 64, 137 (*see also* Lifeboats); maiden voyage of, 22–23; luxury of, 33, 45; materials of, 23; neutrality of questioned, 126; outfitting of, 21; propaganda after sinking and, 138–144; romance on board, 63; sighting of by *U-20*, 85; social activities on board, 60–61; speeds of, 20, 30, 73, 79, 83, 135, 136; survivors, *see Lusitania* (survivors); torpedoes and, *see Lusitania* (torpedoes and); turbines and, 146; victims, *see Lusitania* (victims); warnings received by, 72, 79; water required for engines, 23; wreck of, *see Lusitania* (wreck of)

Lusitania (sinking of), belowdecks at torpedo impact, 99; causes of, 13, 14; causes of, theories about, 190, 194; coal dust and, 194–195, *195*; communication on board during, 101; conspiracy and, *see* Conspiracy; death of passengers in sea, 108, *111*; debris from, 105; descent of, *92–93*, 110; description of, 13, 92–100, 108; duration of, 108; memorial services for, *129, 130–131*; moment of, 108; number of explosions on remembered, 14; passengers during sinking, 95, 98, 100; possible causes of, 190; U. S. response to, 123, 124, 143, 190

Lusitania (survivors of), condition of, 111–112; folk myth about, 113; memories of sinking of, 14, 138–140; numbers of, 13, 198–199, *200*; photos of, *114–115, 122–123*

Lusitania (torpedoes and), 13, 14, 127; explosion of described, 87, 89, 90–91, 195; first sighting of, 87; size of torpedo hole on, 91

Lusitania (victims of), 148; Americans among, 13, 116, 117, 124; burial of, *128–130*; drowned, appearance of, 112–113, 115; famous, 116; identification of, 113, 116; memorial services for, *130–131*; memorial statue, *201*; numbers of, 10, 198–200

Lusitania (wreck of), bow on, *157*; bridge on, 152; condition of, 144, 147, 148, 149, 151, *155–193*; debris on, 152, 189; depth bomb found on, 152; depth of, 10, 151; docking bridge on, *183*; engine room on, *187*; exploration of, 144–189; first sighting of, 146; fishing nets snagged on, 148, 149, 152, 167, *174*, 189; foredeck on, *167*; lifeboat davit on, *174*; location of, 144; mainmast on, *181*; position of, 14; preservation order and, 203; props and rudder on, *184–185*; shower on, *172*; skylight on, *181*; vents on, *169*; water tanks on, *171*; whistle on, *168*

M

Mackworth, Sir Humphrey, 29, *29*, 45

Mackworth, Margaret, 28, *28*, 29, 41, 60, 81, 87; divorce of, 30, 200; during sinking, 92–95, 98, 105; edits *Time and Tide*, 200; marriage and, 29, 82; suffragette activities of, 45; survival of, 111–112, 115, 116

MacLaren, Sir Charles, 21

Marschall, Ken, 16, 189

Mason, Leslie, 35; death of, 116; during sinking, 102

Mason, Stewart, 35, 102; death of, 116

Mauretania, 100, *196*, *197*; conversion of from coal to oil, 197; convertability into warship of, 20, 203; evades torpedo, 197; first launch of, 196; speed of, 20; year scrapped, 197

Mayer, Judge Julius M., 136, 137, *137*

Medea, 15, 144, 146

Merchantmen, concealed guns on, 64, 74, *75*

Mersey, Lord, 132, 133, 194

Mines, more frequent than torpedoes, 70

Ministry of Defence (British), 15

Morgan, J. Pierpont, 18

Morton, John (deckhand), 81, 87, 99, 116

Morton, Leslie (deckhand), 81, 82, 83; during sinking, 104; first to sight torpedo, 87, 164; search for brother by, 99, 113, 116

N

Naiad, 81

National Gallery (Dublin), 203

Nemo, Captain, 151

New York, 13, 18, 23, 24, 25, 28, 30, 37, 203

New York, 30

New York Times, 23, 31, 124; interviews Captain Turner, 137; reports sinking, *120*

New York Yankees, 31

Newcastle-upon-Tyne, 20

Newspapers, reports of sinking in, *120–121*, 123, 126

Northern Horizon, 17, 144, 146, 148

O

Oceaneering International, 14
Old Head of Kinsale (Ireland),
    10, 79, 132, 134; proximity
    to of *Lusitania* when sunk,
    10, 87, 100, 127, 134
Olympic, 100, 137
Orkney Islands, 38

P

Passchendaele, 126
Pearl, Audrey, 101, 103, 202; sur-
    vival of, 200
Pearl, Stuart, 102, 103, 200
Pearl, Surgeon-Major, 101
Peskett, Leonard, 20
Peter Pan, 116
Philistine, The (magazine), 35
Plankton, 152
Potash and Perlmutter, 116
Preservation (of *Lusitania*), Irish
    government and, 203
Propaganda, after *Lusitania* sunk,
    138–144

Q

Q-ships (armed decoys), 75;
    see also Merchantmen
Queensbury, Marquis of, 132
Queenstown (Cobh, Ireland),
    72, 78, 79, 87, 111, 113,
    116, 117, 130, *198–199*,
    200, 201, 203
Quinn, Thomas (*Lusitania*
    lookout), 87, 164

R

Recruiting (military), *Lusitania*
    sinking and effect on, 140,
    141, 142
Remington Company, ammunition
    on board *Lusitania*, 27
Rice, Spring, 194
Roosevelt, Theodore, views on
    sinking, 118
Rotterdam, 30
Royal Flying Corps, 36
Royal Naval Air Service, 36
Royal Navy, 18, 39, 60, 67, 68,
    128, 194; fear of U-boats and,
    71; found not liable for
    sinking, 135–136
Rubens, paintings by on board
    Lusitania, 203
Russia, 38

S

Saboteurs, 61
St. Paul's Cathedral, size of and
    Lusitania contrasted, 29
St. Thomas (Ontario), 35
Saks, 93
Sauder, Bill, 16, *16*
Sauder, Eric, 16, *16*, 189
Schwieger, Lieutenant Walther
    (*U-20* commander), 38, *38*,
    64, 74, 77, 78, 81, 108, 124,
    128, 134, 136, 190; attack of
    Lusitania by, 90; death of, 203;
    depiction of in propaganda
    film, 143
Scotland, 28, 38
Seattle, 28
Second Class, dining room, 45, *54*;
    ladies' drawing room, *55*;
    lounges, 45, *55*; menu, *54*;
    number of passengers, 37;
    promenade deck, *55*
Shetland Islands, 38
Shipping, neutral, risk to in
    war, 124
Smith, Sir Frederick (Earl of
    Birkenhead), 132
Smith, Sarah, 98, 104
Somme, 126
Sonar, 144, 146, 149
Sphere, The (magazine), 28
Spurr, Cyril, 194

Staten Island Ferry, 29

Stealth Bomber, 146

Storstad, 113

Stowaways, 61, 63, 99

Submarines, 30, 68–69; traditional rules of war and, 76; *see also* U-boats

Suffragettes, 45

Sullivan, Florence (Flor), 45, 77; at moment of torpedo impact, 90

Sullivan, Julia, 45, 77; at moment of torpedo impact, 90; baggage found and returned to, 203; survives, 127

Sun (Baltimore), response to sinking, 123

Swan Hunter and Wigham Richardson Shipyards, 20

T

Third Class, cabin, *36, 58*; description of, 46; dining room, *56–57*; functionality of, 46, 56; ladies' sitting room, *57*; number of passengers, 37; plainness of, 45, *56–57*; smoking room, *57*

Thomas, D. A. (David), *28, 29*; survival of, 116–117

Time and Tide, 200

Times (London), response to sinking, 123

Tirpitz, Amiral Alfred von, *68;* U-boats and, 68, 69, 71

Titanic, 13, 16, 32, 113, 137, 144; lifeboats on, 63, 132; losses on, 200

Titian, paintings by on board *Lusitania*, 203

Torpedoes, evasion of, *see* Zigzagging; firing of described, 84–85; inefficiency of, 65, 190; less frequent than mines, 70; rate of misfiring of, 65

Tower, Frank (mythical survivor), 113

Transylvania, guns on board, 79

Turbinia, 197

Turner (mythical survivor), *113*

Turner, Norman, 31

Turner, Percy, 31

Turner, Captain William, *29, 78, 202*; accused of negligence, 194; age of, 30; at moment of torpedo impact, 90; death of, 202, 203; commands other ships, 137; description of after sinking, 127; exoneration of, 137; failure of, 104; gives up hope, 101; ignores Admiralty orders on U-boats, 79; knowledge of sea of, 30; opinion of submarines, 30, 133; personality of, 30, 134, 203; social duties of, 59; survival of, 112, *127*; survives other sinking, 137; treatment of by passengers, 59; uneasy about crew, 59; warned to stay away from land, 82; willingness to go down with ship, 105; witness at inquiries, 133–135; zigzagging and, 133–134, 136; *see also* Zigzagging

Twenty Thousand Leagues Under the Sea (Verne), 151

U

Uncle Sam, in propaganda, 141

U. S. State Department, 194

U. S., does not join war because of *Lusitania*, 15; opinion of British of, 125; opinion of Germans after sinking, 125, 143; war with Germany and, 136

U-9, 70; sinks *Aboukir, Cressy, Hogue*, 70

U-17, sinks *Glitra*, 71

U-20, destruction of, 203; misfiring torpedoes on, 65; morale of crew of, 64, 81; propaganda and, 139, 143; route of, 37–38, *39, 65*; sighting of *Lusitania* by, 85; sinking of *Lusitania* by, 85, 90, 136; sinks *Candidate*, 74; sinks *Centurion*, 77; sinks *Earl of Lathom*, 74; top speed of, 83

U-24, depiction of in propaganda, *142*

U-88, 203

U-boats, Admiralty instructions about, 79, 134; attack techniques of, 80; conditions on, 38–39; destroyers and, 64; early disappointments of, 69; name explained, 69; number of ships sunk by, 78; periscope of, 83; procedures for avoiding, 128, 133–134; vulnerability of on surface, *75*, 80; *see also* Submarines; Zigzagging

Ultonia, 137

Unterseeboot, see U-boats

V

Vancouver, 28

Vanderbilt, Alfred Gwynne, 32, *33*, 59; death of, 116, 164; during sinking, 102; mysterious message received by, 32, 37; personality of, 32

Vanderbilt, Commodore, 32

Vanderbilt, Elsie, 32

Verdun, 126

Verne, Jules, 151

W

Wainsborough, District Inspector, 127

Wales, 41

Weather, 63

Webb, Captain Richard, 194

Weddigen, Lieutenant Otto (*U-9* commander), 70, *70*, 71

Westminster Abbey, 130

Westminster Hall, 133

White Star Line, 13, 18, 74

Wilde, Oscar, 132

Wilhelm, Kaiser, 35, 67, *68*, 152; in propaganda, 138, 141

Williams, Annie, 36

Williams, David, 36

Williams, Edith, 36, 100, *202*; survival of, 110–111, *162*, 200

Williams, Edward, 36, *202*; survival of, 200

Williams, Ethel, 36

Williams, Florence, 36, 100, 110

Williams, George, 36

Williams, John, 36, 200

Wilson, President Woodrow, 60, 123, *124*; warns Germans, 124–125

Y

Yoerger, Dana, 16

Z

Zigzagging, not used by *Lusitania*, 127, 128, 133–134, 136

Design and Art Direction: Gordon Sibley Design Inc.

Editorial Director: Hugh Brewster

Project Editor: Ian R. Coutts

Editorial Assistance: Lloyd Davis
Shelley Tanaka

Production Director: Susan Barrable

Production Coordinator: Sandra L. Hall

Original Paintings: Ken Marschall

Maps and Diagrams: Jack McMaster

Color Separation: Colour Technologies

Printing And Binding: Arnoldo Mondadori S.p.A.

Exploring the Lusitania
was produced by Madison Press Books under the
direction of Albert E. Cummings